FORBIDDEN BEAT

FORBIDDEN BEAT
perspectives on punk drumming

Edited by S. W. Lauden

RARE BIRD
Los Angeles, Calif.

THIS IS A GENUINE RARE BIRD BOOK

Rare Bird Books
453 South Spring Street, Suite 302
Los Angeles, CA 90013
rarebirdbooks.com

FIRST TRADE PAPERBACK EDITION

For more information, address:
Rare Bird Books Subsidiary Rights Department
453 South Spring Street, Suite 302
Los Angeles, CA 90013

Set in Minion
Printed in the United States

Cover artwork by Brian Walsby

10 9 8 7 6 5 4 3 2 1

Library of Congress Cataloging-in-Publication Data
Names: Lauden, S. W., editor.
Title: Forbidden beat : perspectives on punk drumming /
edited by S. W. Lauden.
Description: First hardcover edition. | Los Angeles, CA : Rare Bird Books,
2022. | Includes bibliographical references.
Identifiers: LCCN 2021044890 | ISBN 9781644282274 (trade paperback)
Subjects: LCSH: Punk rock music—History and criticism. | Punk rock
musicians. | Drummers (Musicians) | Punk rock musicians—Interviews. |
Drummers (Musicians)—Interviews.
Classification: LCC ML3534 .F664 2022 | DDC 782.4216609—dc23

LC record available at https://lccn.loc.gov/2021044890

CONTENTS

FOREWORD

By Lucky Lehrer

YOU CANNOT LOVE PUNK music without loving punk drummers. Punk's early drummers were pistons, providing a pulse that drove the music. They rebelled against extravagant drum sets overloaded with cymbals and toms, in favor of stripped-down kits. Less-is-more drummers including K. K. Barrett of the Screamers, the first punk band I ever saw because my friend Paul Roessler happened to be the keyboardist, illustrate that the most dramatic move in music is the simple rest note. Silence is what allows notes to echo and breathe.

Looking back, the Screamers were more of an art band than a punk band. There was no uniform sound for early punk bands, but they were often lumped together in their nihilism under the nebulous phrase "new wave." This kind of misses the point since punk was all about self-expression. Drummer El Duce of the Mentors offers an outstanding example of punk drummer as artist. He crafted a uniquely colorful kit where no drum, no cymbal, and no stand were the same color or the same brand. His drum set appears to have been found in trash cans, at pawn shops, and from flea market finds. Even El Duce's right and left drumsticks were different!

When I first started playing drums on punk rock's low stages—seldom were risers used, offering a better the view of drummers—I assembled a combination of fiberglass drums with North brand tom-toms to deliver maximum volume. Drums were rarely mic'd at early Circle Jerks gigs (garage soirées and birthday parties). Those drums contributed to the sound on the band's breakout album from 1980, *Group Sex*.

Irrespective of the particulars of chosen equipment, there is a collective lack of self-consciousness among punk drummers. Where a serious drummer may warm up backstage with rolls and ratamacues on a practice pad, a punk drummer might prepare by guzzling a fifth of Jack Daniel's—and then storm the stage like wildfire.

There were four genres of pop music on FM radio when I graduated University High School in West Los Angeles in the mid-seventies along with Paul Roessler, Darby Crash of the Germs, and Pat Smear of the Germs (later the Foo Fighters) to name just a few of whom would go on to completely change the musical landscape. As a mutant offshoot of glam, punk music began oozing through vacant basements and dank art venues, including Brendan Mullen's underground hellhole, The Masque, in Hollywood. In the media, music critic Lester Bangs who wrote for *Creem* and *Rolling Stone* referred to the Midwest's MC5 and Iggy Pop as punks. To distinguish its cadence, Ira Elliot observes in the first chapter of *Forbidden Beat* that punk music's drumbeats were fabricated to upend convention.

The Ramones were aware of the MC5 and Iggy Pop. Their first drummer, Tommy Ramone, was a guitarist who had never played the drums before joining the band. Some punk drummers did have formal training (D. J. Bonebrake of X comes to mind. D. J. is a proficient sight reader who can play vibes and marimba). Tommy's beats—simple bass and snare patterns, with his right stick on the hi-hat and never a tom-tom fill—are the Ramones' sound. Over time, the Ramones had several drummers. Each stayed true to Tommy's style. Each had the stamina to plow through thirty fast songs with no time to catch their breath.

As Curt Weiss points out in chapter two of *Forbidden Beat*, punk drumming should not be confused with a lack of creativity. Savvy dissidents, punk drummers were inventive in their defiance. The band Fear's drummer (and a personal favorite), Spit Stix, crossed between his snare drum and a used oil barrel in "We Destroy the Family." His driving beat sounds ominous and intense.

My personal journey began in elementary school and married the ferocity of big band, up tempo swing with overtones of the Latin clave. I borrowed from the Mitzvah bands I used to play in as a kid; my yarmulke-wielding side hustle. Oom-pah standards like "Hava Nagila" (which literally means "Let Us Rejoice") emphasize the down beat and inspired what's now called the "forbidden beat." In an arms race for originality, John Robb states in chapter three that early punk drummers created a completely new rhythmic language. Topper Headon of the Clash was so innovative that rap musicians still sample his beats today.

It's easier to hear a killer drum beat than it is to use words to describe it. The challenge to verbally explain syncopation did not discourage Matt Diehl from dissecting the D-beat. Along with drummers Daniel Glass and Spike T. Smith's prior historical research, Diehl traces another of punk's most often used rhythms. The classic D-beat is known for a "grinding, distorted, and brutally political sound." With the cymbal playing and snare drum cracking rim shots on two and four, the beat puts the bass drum on one and plays the "ands" of two and three. A good example of how this beat sounds is John Maher's drumming on the Buzzcocks' song "You Tear Me Up," and Tezz Roberts on Discharge's first EP, *Realities of War*.

Forbidden Beat is not only a book for drummers. Musicians and music fans will gain a finer appreciation for songcraft by discovering how punk drummers develop memorable music. The authors did not intend an exhaustive compendium on the "world's greatest punk drummers." Some influential contributors to punk's pantheon of percussionists from Paul Cook to Travis Barker are discussed. Some noteworthy players aren't mentioned. Chapters are based on what the individual contributors decided to write about. So, if your favorite drummer's name doesn't appear in this book, don't fret. The idea behind this is to throw a spotlight on drummers everywhere. I applaud every kid who ever bashed a secondhand trap set with shitty cymbals and a janky kick pedal. We wail and flail in primal exuberance for the sheer joy of it.

I gained a lot by reading an advance copy of *Forbidden Beat*. Phanie Diaz, the drummer from Fea, reminded me of how much I learned from closely watching other drummers play. When I started, things like surfing, skateboarding, and playing drums were considered "boy things." There were a few female drummers, but what used to be a novelty has thankfully spawned several greats whose stories appear in the book, including Gina Schock, Lori Barbero, and Lynn Perko-Truell, among many others. As drummers, we may be happy with our playing, but never totally satisfied. There's an infinite number of ideas, techniques, different genres, and new gear to become familiar with.

As the pages in my left (back beat) hand became thicker, I realized I was sadly nearing the end of this book. The stories conclude with a great interview with Rat Scabies from the Damned. Back to 1976: Rat, Brian James, Dave Vanian, and Captain Sensible appeared with a sound and look that felt excitingly different.

I agree with Rat that among early jazz drummers, Gene Krupa was totally amazing, and Buddy Rich was absolutely terrifying. No two drummers play the same, and that is the best part of it.

Drummers march armies into war. Before they are born, babies hear their mother's heartbeat in what might be called a *Bossa Nova in-utero*. Drumbeats are felt in the soul and heard in the heart. There is something primitive about pounding drums we drummers feel called to do. Whether an African Djembe, a "Bata" used in religious ceremonies, the latest electronic drum pads, or a simple wooden crate that today is marketed as a Cajón, banging out rhythms just feels good. Drum machines may sound realistic, robots can be programmed to play drums, and with Pro Tools (recording software that converts music to dots and dashes), you can do anything.

Black Flag's famous vocalist Henry Rollins said on TV that a band is only as good as its drummer. It is worth remembering, as Curt Weiss points out in his essay about Jerry Nolan, that we punk drummers may play like jack hammers, but we are not machines. Whatever the song, no matter the tempo, find your groove, play the pocket, swing the band, strive for tone, keep improving, and have fun.

Lucky Lehrer *performed and recorded with several LA bands including the Circle Jerks and Bad Religion. He appears in major films, charting the rise of punk rock music. Considered influential by Dave Grohl, Travis Barker, Dave Lombardo, and many others, Lehrer was voted one of the best punk drummers of all time.*

INTRODUCTION

By S. W. Lauden

M Y OLDER BROTHERS FED me a steady diet of heavy metal and classic rock as a kid, so punk rock was the first music that felt like mine. My mind was repeatedly blown, and my life was changed when I first discovered bands like the Ramones, Sex Pistols, Dead Kennedys, X, Hüsker Dü, and Fugazi. I grew to embrace many other genres over the years, but I've always considered punk rock the gateway into my own musical exploration and self-expression.

Although I'm a drummer who counts Paul Cook, D. J. Bonebrake, Grant Hart, and Bill Stevenson among my many influences, I approached this book more as a reader and fan. There is no shortage of excellent books about punk rock available, and quite a few impressive collections about drumming, but to my knowledge there has never been a book that specifically explored the fascinating universe of punk drummers from across the decades. So, I decided to put one together with the help of some truly talented contributors. (Seriously, look at that table of contents!) Lucky for us, there was a lot of material to work with.

Depending on your definition of the genre, punk rock has been around in some form for over fifty years—but *Forbidden Beat* is definitely more of a celebration than an exhaustive history.

This collection is designed to shine the spotlight on the thrashing, crashing hearts of our favorite punk bands as selected by each contributor. The perspectives and opinions on punk drumming shared in these pages are directly from people who love and respect it, have experienced it up close and personal, or have done it themselves.

Over one hundred and fifty drummers are written about or referenced in this book, from self-taught bashers to technical wizards and just about every style of playing in between. Some have whole chapters dedicated to them, while others are mentioned as important influences in a sentence or two. Taken all together, the diverse viewpoints, opinions, and personal stories included here create a kind of collage that hopefully connects the rhythmic dots for many different eras, scenes, and bands.

Along the way, I'm confident you will discover a few new-to-you punk drummers or gain insights on some old favorites— but we're still only scratching the surface. That means that some of your hard-hitting heroes have undoubtedly been left out. Understand that this had more to do with the constraints of space and time than bias, ignorance, or spite. And, hey, there's always the chance that we'll put together a second volume.

If you've made it this far, I hope you'll enjoy these essays, interviews, and lists encompassing sixties garage rock, first wave seventies punk, eighties hardcore, nineties Riot grrrl and pop punk, and onto punk drumming in the 2000s. More than anything, this collection is a salute to that sweaty blur at the back of the stage giving everything to propel the music we love.

So, grab those sticks and count it off...*one-two-three-four!*

S. W. Lauden *is the coeditor of* Go All The Way: Literary Appreciations of Power Pop *and the sequel,* Go Further. *His Greg Salem punk rock PI series includes* Bad Citizen Corporation, Grizzly Season, *and* Hang Time. *Steve's a father, husband, writer, and drummer living in Los Angeles. More at swlauden.com.*

STRAIGHT EIGHTHS FROM THE GARAGE

By Ira Elliot

I'M THE DRUMMER IN the opening band. The five of us—two guitarists, a bassist, a keyboard player, and I—occupy the thin strip of space between the headline act's amplifiers and the monitors at the lip of the stage. And although this was a fairly big stage in a good-sized ballroom, we still had to get my drum kit, four amps, and a keyboard up there with us, so we were pretty cozy.

Whatever happened to one of us, happened to all of us. So, when someone in the audience spat at us somewhere in the middle of the first song, I watched mostly in bemusement. Sitting tucked behind the other four, I was farthest away and hardest to hit. One of the small, unspoken benefits of being a drummer, really. Harder to hit with spit.

As the show progressed so did the number of spitters and frequency of the spitting. I'd watch these little white flecks launching upward from the dark, near distance in front of us. Like little incoming comets, they lit up brightly as they flew into the atmosphere of the stage lights. If you were on your game, you could easily shift your body out of the slow-motion arc homing in on you.

This is what it was like to open for the Damned in the eighties. One of the many things that I didn't know about the Damned at the time was that their drummer, the subtly named Rat Scabies, was the guy who invented "gobbing" (as they say in jolly gross England). It turns out that during a moment in early punk history, the British press, always on the lookout for horrible things to report about the excessive and antiestablishment behavior of the country's disaffected youth, filed a report from some gig where they witnessed an audience member (one R. Scabies) hocking up clams at his friends in the Sex Pistols as they bashed away. So the next day when it hit the tabloids it became the most punk thing to do.

So, it follows that the very same audience who spat at us during our thirty-minute opening slot continued to do so, wildly and enthusiastically, throughout the ninety-plus minutes of the Damned's show, as well. That was the summer of 1985 when I was playing with the Fuzztones. In the early eighties, we were part of a New York garage rock revival scene along with bands like the Chesterfield Kings, the Fleshtones, and the A-Bones. But similar bands were popping up around the country back then with the Pandoras, the Three O'Clock, Rain Parade, the Dream Syndicate, the Bangles, and the Long Ryders in California; Plan 9 from Rhode Island; the Miracle Workers in Oregon; R.E.M. from Georgia; Lyres from Massachusetts; and the Cynics from Pennsylvania—to name but a few.

When I joined the Fuzztones in 1983, I found myself in a community of garage rock life-stylers. Folks with amazing Prince Valiant haircuts, new old stock striped Haggar slacks from 1965, rocket ship-shaped sixties Italian bass guitars and vast garage rock album collections. It was a small but very eclectic scene that drew some really unique characters. It's not head music, it's soul music, and the audiences who came to hear these bands were looking for the catharsis that only a hot rock and roll band in a small, crowded room can invoke. The thing that connects a band on a stage to the people watching and listening is something primal.

What I didn't fully comprehend that evening in 1985 at the Barrowlands in Glasgow opening for the Damned was that the music my band played—songs from little-known regional American garage bands of the sixties—was a core inspiration for seventies punk.

◆

FROM A DRUMMER'S PERSPECTIVE, fifties rock and roll was characterized by the shuffle. Early blues, country, and swing were all predicated on this simple musical duplet, but something else was happening as well—a new reliance on straighter eighth notes. Broadly speaking, this shift from swung eighth notes to straight eighth notes is the central rhythmic shift that defines modern music in the last half of the twentieth century.

This more aggressive straight-eighth feel was often placed directly against the shuffle. In arrangements like "Roll Over Beethoven" and "Sweet Little Sixteen," Chuck Berry and his band are delivering a hybrid. The drummer, Fred Below, doesn't give much away. His feel is intractable and tends to emphasize a very straight four with the snare and kick allowing space for the guitar and piano to spar between straight and swung eighths; however, you can still make out a subtle swing on the ride cymbal.

Chuck would sing and play hard eighth notes for one section while shifting into a more swinging feel in another on songs like "Rock and Roll Music." But the guys who did this best were piano players like Little Richard and Jerry Lee Lewis, who could really lean in on the hard eighth feels. "Lucille," "Keep A-Knockin'," and "Good Golly, Miss Molly"—which all have a ton of swing in them—also feature harder eighth notes either in the rhythm section or the vocals line.

This rhythmic contrast is thrilling because it gives the listener the impression that things are just about to completely fly off the rails. So, it was only natural for young rock and roll bands in the early sixties to lean more heavily on straight eighths. And that's when the Sonics show up in Tacoma, Washington.

◆

THE SONICS, LIKE MANY local bands in the Pacific Northwest, were a teen dance band specializing in raved-up soul, R&B, and rock and roll—both covers and originals. They stand out because of their menacing recordings, two tracks with one mic above the kit producing a sound that's like a controlled explosion. Pure teenage adrenaline with all needles in the red. Nineteen sixty-five's *Here Are The Sonics!* is undoubtedly, pound for pound, one of the greatest rock and roll albums ever made.

Their drummer, Bob Bennett's style turns on a few very basic elements. Most of the heavy lifting is done by laying hard, backbeat rimshots across his cranked-up snare, which—along with the single mic recording—really makes the drums jump. His sixteenth-note machine gun rolls are plentiful and satisfying every time, even though they all seem to go just one bit too fast. But everything always lands perfectly and is anchored by his tendency to play straight eighths on the kick. Punchy. Brutal. Primitive. Which is why it always seemed right to refer to the Sonics as "proto punk," because to me it sounds like something they found in an archeological dig.

And so, by the late sixties, tougher straight eighths became the perfect backbeat for bands taking an artistic stand against the sunny idealism of the hippies. In New York City in 1967, that band was the Velvet Underground. Formed primarily as a house band for Andy Warhol's Factory crowd, they soon became a vehicle for Lou Reed's hard-boiled, Raymond Chandler-esque songs of excess. And their drummer, Moe Tucker—a completely self-taught amateur with no previous experience—became, by that very nature, an important influence on legions of drummers to follow. Rock critic Robert Christgau once said of Tucker, "Moe was a great drummer in a minimalist, limited, autodidactic way that I think changed musical history. She is where the punk notion of how the beat works begins."

What did he mean by the "punk notion of how the beat works"? I believe he's saying that the punk drumming ethos revolved around bare-bones minimalism and an animating primitivism. This is a very central point. Moe Tucker's style is tribal. She chose, for example, to flip the kick drum over, batter head up, so she could stand and play the kick, snare, toms, and tambourine (no cymbals!) with just mallets in her hands. Listen to the simple pounding of "I'm Waiting for the Man." It's just a pulse really, perfect for a song about intravenous drug use, but it's absolutely mesmerizing. Especially as the whole band is pulsing out eighth notes together. Where the guitar solo would normally go, there's just more hypnotic rhythm. The song defies you not to play it again when it ends. One more fix.

"Venus in Furs," a dark song about an equally perverse subject, is somberly anchored by the ominous one-two of bass drum and tambourine. It's the perfect stark backdrop for this severe little scene. "Run Run Run" is a rocking shuffle again simply pounded out on a bass drum with mallets. This softer, amateurish approach clearly runs contrary to the classic, hard-rocking drummer paradigm, and the average drummer might not see the appeal of her playing, but that's why it was called punk rock. Its creativity was fueled by defying convention.

◆▶

IN 1968, YOUNG DETROIT native Iggy Pop went to check out the Doors, who were playing a graduation concert at the University of Michigan. He thought Jim Morrison had an amazing presence—moody, dangerous, transgressive, outlaw—but he hated the other three guys. He came away firmly convinced that the band he had just formed in Ann Arbor, the Stooges, could do much better. And if you ask me, he was dead right.

The Stooges' drummer, Scott Asheton was, at his best, a brutal minimalist, his simple rhythms revolving in mesmerizing two- and four-bar phrases. "1969" is a non-stop, lopsided Bo Diddley beat that is tribal and primitive. The funky, Detroit swagger of "No Fun" is the soundtrack to the Stooges walking down the street like Tony Manero in *Saturday Night Fever*. And if you've ever wondered how to make sleigh bells sound menacing, you'll find the answer in the druggy, sexed-up freak beat of "I Wanna Be Your Dog."

The greatness of these beats becomes clear when you perform them yourself. They're fairly easy to play and totally hypnotic. All you have to do is not speed up or slow down. Linear. Droning. No fills. And if you're a drummer like me—programmed by years of repetition to make some kind of extra-rhythmic comment at the end of every phrase—actively choosing to play nothing is an act of concentration and will. You need to train yourself to do it. Or not do it, as the case may be.

The Stooges were discovered by record label guys who had come to Detroit to sign their friends' band, MC5. Their drummer, Dennis Thompson, is often referred to as a "wild man" and watching live footage of MC5 from back in the day bears this out. He is clearly the American Keith Moon. He plays with an animal aggression, which is both highly propulsive and teetering on the edge of "completely-out-of-control." But while MC5 undoubtedly

21

radiated a manic energy, they were wired up tight. With stop/start arrangements and careening guitar solos played ferociously but with focus, this was not a droning art-school experiment. It was a tightly clenched rock and roll fist to the teeth.

Which brings us back to New York. An acolyte of Gene Krupa, Jerry Nolan was a natural showman. By 1972, a well-known New York scenester with a notoriously well-developed sense of style in a city full of style monsters, he joined the New York Dolls after the tragic death of their first drummer, Billy Murcia. Nolan was right at home behind the ragged, fabulous front line of David Johansen, Johnny Thunders, Sylvain Sylvain and Arthur Kane—all posing and staggering around on heels or drugs or both. With his thumpy, oversized, hot pink kit, he was a forceful pounder who held the whole anarchic party together.

But it all comes together with the Ramones. Joey Ramone was the drummer when the band first formed in Queens in 1974, but good fortune quickly put Joey up front and Tommy Erdelyi (a.k.a. Tommy Ramone) behind the kit. While many might equate Marky as the Ramones drummer, Tommy defined the minimalist, compressed style on those first three albums that became the overarching aesthetic for all future Ramones recordings (and countless punk bands around the world).

Tommy was a guitarist who, up until the point when he joined the band, had *never played drums before.* Yet he got the gig because he inherently understood how the drums needed to function in Ramones' arrangements. A relentless and single-dynamic straight line which, because it called little attention to itself, allowed you to better enjoy the Ramones' most powerful weapon—Joey's remarkable voice and those pop-perfect melodies.

But the other quality the Ramones exemplified—one that isn't generally associated with the free-floating, I-don't-care discontent of punk rock—was a military discipline in arrangement and stagecraft. Ramones shows were wired breathtakingly tight like few bands you can imagine. Most songs hardly ended before Dee Dee yelled his notorious, tempo-irrespective ONETWOTHREEFOUR! and you had better know what the next song was before he got to TWO. The Ramones were the proverbial well-oiled machine and Tommy's simple, no bullshit style was the engine that drove it.

When I first heard my hometown band the Ramones on the radio, it sounded both alien and familiar. I didn't really see, maybe even until right now as I'm writing this, how the Ramones effectively synthesized the attitude of the Dolls, the discipline of MC5, the aggression of the Stooges, the simplicity of the Velvet Underground, and the teenage energy of the Sonics. I can't imagine what the world would be like if they hadn't.

The wild, primitive rock and roll impulse—the urge to set a beat in motion and set a room on fire—this is the drummer's charge. And the original spark for generations of punk drummers has always been those straight eighth beats that came from the garage.

Ira Elliot *is and has been the drummer in Nada Surf for the past twenty-five years but has known the other members of the band for thirty-five years since he was a member, and they were fans of The Fuzztones. He lives with his lovely wife, Jen, and daughter, Vivian, in sunny, Sarasota, Florida.*

MAXIMIZE THE MINIMAL & LET IT SWING

By Curt Weiss

I HAVE VIVID MEMORIES of walking through an outdoor arts and crafts fair as an adolescent. As my sister and I went from table to table, I pointed at different knickknacks and *objets d'art* repeatedly saying, "I can do that." One table I was particularly struck by was covered in stick figures made of welded nuts, bolts, washers, and screws. After hearing "I can do that" more times than he could stand, the artist grabbed my pudgy hand, looked me in the eye, and said, "The point is, you didn't." Years later I realized that what I was looking at was a form of minimalism. Any of us could have created minimalist pieces like John Cage's "4'33," Andy Warhol's "Sleep," or Mark Rothko's "Orange, Red, Yellow," but unless you are the reincarnated Cage, Warhol, or Rothko, you didn't.

Rock and roll is often a form of minimalism. A song may only have three chords in total, a few recurring melodies, fragmentary lyrics, and simple, repetitive rhythms, all played with a high level of passion and energy as opposed to a high level of virtuosity. That music would not only be minimalist, but often be punk rock.

The origins of punk rock have been debated since the movement first appeared in the seventies. A number of unpolished and primitive sources exist—the rawest and simplest rock and roll from early rockers like Little Richard, Buddy Holly, or Screamin' Jay Hawkins; the distorted guitar sounds of Link Wray; fifties rockabilly hepcats Johnny Burnette, Gene Vincent, Eddie Cochran, or any number of artists Sam Phillips discovered in Memphis (Howlin' Wolf, Elvis, Jerry Lee Lewis, Carl Perkins); sixties garage rock *Nuggets* made by the likes of the 13th Floor Elevators, the Kingsmen, the Seeds, and the Electric Prunes; the primal Brit-boom records of the Kinks, the Troggs, and the Who; the art rock of David Bowie and Roxy Music; and the working-class boot-stomping glam of Mott the Hoople and Slade. But if ground zero for punk rock is the handful of bands who came to prominence at New York's CBGB in 1974/75 (Television with Richard Hell, the Ramones, the Patti Smith Group, Blondie) and the scene in and around London in 1975/76 (Sex Pistols, Buzzcocks, the Clash, the Damned, Siouxsie and the Banshees), there are a number of groups who overlapped from previous genres and movements who were key influences for those groups: Tacoma, Washington's the Sonics; New York City-based[1] the Velvet Underground; Detroit, Michigan's MC5, as well as Ann Arbor's the Stooges; Boston, Massachusetts' the Modern Lovers; and two groups from the outer boroughs of New York City, the unfairly ignored Dictators, and the band that won the award as both best and worst new group in the 1973 *Creem Magazine* readers poll, New York Dolls.

Outside of the Dictators, whose influence lay more in their pre-Ramones embrace of teenage rebellion for the hell of it meets junk food/TV culture, the drummers in each of these groups (Bob Bennett with the Sonics, Moe Tucker with the Velvets, Dennis Thompson with MC5, Scott Asheton with the Stooges, and David Robinson with the Modern Lovers) were a vital part of

---

1   While The Velvet Underground formed in New York City, viola and bassist John Cale was born in Wales, and vocalist Nico hailed from Germany.

the chemistry that not only made them great but inspired many of their listeners to dare make their own music. But the drummer I always felt most drawn to was the owner of those unforgettable baby pink drums, New York Dolls' Jerry Nolan. While I found his flair for fashion, urban hipster idiosyncrasies, and hard-luck story so irresistible that I had to write a book about him, when it got down to brass tacks, it was his drumming that left its most lasting impression on not only me but punk rock.

Taken in its totality, Jerry's punk rock resume is lofty. He played with Johnny Thunders, as influential a guitarist as any to come out of the glam or punk eras. He played with punk originator Richard Hell and punk icon Sid Vicious. He was along for the Anarchy Tour just as punk was spreading out beyond London into every living room in England. He was with the Dolls at the Mercer Arts Center and Max's Kansas City in 1972, and with the Heartbreakers at the first CBGB Underground Rock Festival in 1975. But his impact was felt for years afterward, from the first waves of punk rock and new wave to the pounding drummers of the grunge and alt-rock years.

Jerry became the Dolls' drummer after an extensive series of auditions following the unfortunate death of their first drummer, Billy Murcia, while the band was in England trying to roust up record company interest. Jerry's main competition for the drummer's seat came from Marc Bell, who would go on to play with Richard Hell & the Voidoids on their landmark album *Blank Generation*. In 1978, he'd change his name to "Marky Ramone" after joining the Ramones following the departure of their original drummer Tommy, who left to pursue a career in record production.

Marc, like Jerry, also had a short stint backing transgender singer Jayne County. But during the Dolls auditions, Bell played much like he did while in Dust, a more conventional hard rock band he played with who put out two albums in the early seventies. Bell acknowledges that he blew his chance to be a Doll by overplaying, showing off his fluency in different time signatures and playing John Bonham-style triplet combinations. Stylistically, it did not work with the Dolls as well as Jerry's simpler approach.

While Bell's contribution to *Blank Generation* is top notch, it should be viewed through a "post-punk" as opposed to a "punk" lens. Hell was now leading his third band in as many years, and purposefully shunned the rougher style of early Television or the rawness of the pre-*L.A.M.F.* Heartbreakers. Instead, Hell chose to surround himself with more experienced players, the uniquely accomplished guitar duo of Robert Quine and Ivan Julian, as well as the equally gifted Bell, while Hell played bass and sang his own songs. When Bell again attempted a more minimalist style with the Ramones, he was fortunate to have their first drummer Tommy give him direct guidance in "dumbing down" his playing. After the experience of his failed Dolls audition, Marc got the message and kept his playing simple with a capital "S."

Though he liked large drums, Jerry always used a small kit—one bass drum, one hanging tom and one, sometimes two, floor toms, one flat ride cymbal and two equally flat crashes to go with his hi-hat. Unlike many popular drummers of the day (the Who's Keith Moon, Yes & King Crimson's Bill Bruford, Led Zeppelin's John Bonham, Emerson, Lake & Palmer's Carl Palmer, the Mahavishnu Orchestra's Billy Cobham), there were no gongs, second bass drum, tympanis, upside-down China cymbals, or multiple racks of tom-toms in his setup. To Jerry, if it was good enough for his idol, swing-era drummer Gene Krupa, it was good enough for him. Like Ringo Starr or Charlie Watts, the smaller kit helped force him to be an economical player, always cognizant of the songs' melodic hook, the main guitar riff, and the lead singer. He never stepped on anyone's solos or missed an accent. If he did anything out of the norm, it was always with the betterment of the song in mind.

Like other first wave punk drummers such as Blondie's Clem Burke or the Sex Pistols' Paul Cook, Jerry also had drive—the ability to propel the music forward and lead the rest of the band in all the twists and turns a song could take. There was no doubt that while his Dolls bandmates Johnny Thunders, David Johansen, and Sylvain Sylvain were working the crowd from the lip of the stage, and bass player Arthur Kane was precariously balanced atop his six-inch platform heels toward the rear by his amp, Jerry was in command of where the songs were headed. Stops, starts, tempos, accents, dynamics—Jerry pointed the way and the rest of them had to follow.

By the time of Jerry's tenure with the Dolls (late 1972 through April of 1975), he'd had over ten years of experience as a drummer. Besides County, he'd played with Ventures-like instrumental combos, Top 40 cover bands, future glam star Suzi Quatro and her sisters in Detroit, exotic dancers at strip clubs, "goosing" jokes with rim shots for Bette Midler, Hendrix covers behind Curtis Knight, and eighties hit maker-to-be Billy Squier—all experiences that afforded him loads of opportunities to become fluent in multiple pop music styles. Jerry learned that drum styles may have something to do with which drum you hit and when, but also come from the proper use of accents, syncopation, and that almost impossible to define element, feel, as opposed to technical dexterity. This was evident on Dolls' tracks like "Stranded in the Jungle," which starts with a tom-tom heavy Bo Diddley-style beat, and transitions to more of a big band Jazz-cum-R&B swing in the choruses. "Showdown" and "Babylon" also have one distinct style in the choruses and another in the verses, with dramatic dynamic flourishes throughout. Even the much-maligned live *Red Patent Leather* recordings contained new songs including the title track, "On Fire," and a roaring cover of Eddie Cochran's "Something Else" that exhibit driving, creative, multifaceted rock and roll drumming.

Jerry's personal influences are apparent throughout both Dolls albums as well as the Heartbreakers' lone LP *L.A.M.F.* "Private World" borrows from the Rolling Stones' Charlie Watts ("My Obsession"). "Babylon" has similarities to Mitch Mitchell's work with the Jimi Hendrix Experience ("I Don't Live Today"). "Trash" from the Dolls' first album, and "Baby Talk" from *L.A.M.F.*, are undoubtedly homages to his hero Gene Krupa ("Sing, Sing, Sing"). First-wave punk groups, including Blondie, the Ramones, the Clash, the Damned, and Sex Pistols, all played on bills with bands Jerry drummed for. All of them contained unapologetic Dolls and Heartbreakers fans. Despite their own multitudes of drumming influences, Blondie's "Kung Fu Girls," the Pistols' "Problems," the Clash's "Janie Jones," and the Damned's "New Rose" all contain characteristics of Jerry Nolan in how their drummers approached these songs. They're concise and driving, contain few frills, are awash with sustained crashing cymbals, are filled with dynamics, and have controlled but limited embellishments. The dictum apparent throughout is "Don't overplay. Compliment."

All of those early punk bands had drummers with character, which added to what was great about them. But arguably they all grew up on the rock and roll of the sixties. Jerry, however, grew up on the sounds of the fifties, and with that he brought swing. Like a jazz player, his ability to swing gave the music a comfortable hop or skip in its feel, as if the hard mechanical edges of rhythm were rounded off and smoothed out. This was evidenced not only by his playing, but by the playing of those who tried to replace him. Both the Damned's Rat Scabies and the Sex Pistols' Paul Cook tried to fill Jerry's shoes for a few gigs when he left the Heartbreakers in October 1977 after the release of their flawed masterpiece *L.A.M.F.* Though they each had their own unique set of skills to offer, according to Heartbreaker Walter Lure, neither could quite cut it on the fifties or pre-Beatles styled songs. That's because while these drummers were brought up on the Who and Small Faces, Jerry was brought up on Frankie Lymon and Cozy Cole. Something like their cover of Gary US Bonds' "Seven Day Weekend" was simply not in their wheelhouse. But to Jerry, it was second nature.

While Jerry only made three studio albums in his career (two with the Dolls and one with the Heartbreakers), his simpler, driving approach stood out from what was commonplace at the time. It worked perfectly for the Dolls, who were also doing something reminiscent of another era—the three-minute pop song. One noted fan was Paul Westerberg of those beautiful losers from Minneapolis, the Replacements. Westerberg recognized that the Dolls' songs were, "classic rock-and-roll because they had beginnings, middles, and ends."[2] He also recognized that the drummer didn't need to be a "Fancy Dan"[3] and imparted this lesson to the 'Mats drummer Chris Mars. They understood that Dolls' songs like "Personality Crisis," which only had three chords, still showed a differentiation between verse and chorus, as well as sections within them. Jerry's fills are minimal throughout this song, only using them to build dynamic climaxes, signaling a change from one section to another. Throughout the 1980s,

2   From "Trouble Boys: The True Story of the Replacements" by Bob Mehr, Da Capo, 2016.

3   Ibid.

'Mats recordings such as "Otto" from their first album, *Sorry Ma, Forgot To Take Out The Trash*, *Hootenanny*'s "Color Me Impressed," *Let It Be*'s "I Will Dare," and *Pleased to Meet Me*'s "I.O.U." have that same propulsive, swinging, economical Jerry Nolan approach, which supports the songs but never overtakes them.

On the other side of the Atlantic in London, the post-punk Psychedelic Furs may have given the impression of being just another Ray Ban-wearing New Wave group with a fixation for black clothing and David Bowie. But they were also New York Dolls fans, which is noticeable in their most popular songs, "Pretty in Pink" and "Love My Way." As refined as these recordings were in comparison to the Dolls, they both contain elements of Jerry's style in their charm. The hi-hat propulsion in the verses that gave way to a tom-tom-based thrust in the chorus tip a more polished hat to "Chinese Rocks" from *L.A.M.F.* or even "Human Being" from *Too Much Too Soon*. But they also showed what might have been, had the Dolls or Heartbreakers ever found a trusted and skilled producer who could tap into what the kids in New York and London saw in them, paying off with their own "All the Young Dudes" or "Anarchy in the UK." Years later, bands such as Bad Religion, Green Day, and Blink-182 brought to light some of the pop sensibilities hidden under the murk of *L.A.M.F.* to find their way to gold records and chart success, but were still able to call themselves "punk."

But minimalism should not be confused with a lack of creativity or intentionality. Jerry's playing was always thought out. Sometimes that process would occur onstage, where inspiration would cause him to rethink what he was playing, creating something new and occasionally even spectacular. But still, like a big band jazz player, he swung, always propelling the band forward, steering the rock and roll ship through whatever came within its path. There's a video worth watching of a show he played in Los Angeles at the Roxy in January of 1987 backing his old comrade Johnny Thunders. On bass is original New York Doll Arthur Kane and Jerry's partner in the Idols and the London Cowboys, Barry Jones, on rhythm. As expected, Jerry's playing is minimal, driving, and swings, but he changes the signature tom-tom part in the chorus of "Chinese Rocks," a song he'd played for over ten years, to a military/Johnny Cash-style train beat on the snare drum. Why? Would you have asked Charlie Parker or Billie Holiday why they did something different from one night to another? To paraphrase Louis Armstrong, it's one of those questions where if you have to ask, you'll never know.

During the same show, they open with a song from Johnny's solo period called "Blame it on Mom." Throughout the song there are spots where Jerry strikes four accents on the snare drum. His left arm curves in the air with a ballerina's grace, morphing with the spirit of Gene Krupa, while his head bobs up and down to the groove he's given everyone else to glide upon. All the while he's playing one of the simplest rock and roll beats there is. No recording of this song with any other drummer has ever sounded as thrilling. Such was the impact of Jerry Nolan.

Like a man from a different time and place, dozens of bands took Jerry's ideas and used them to find success while his career always seemed to stall. Less than a year after his compadre Johnny Thunders died in 1991, Jerry's life also ended at the relatively young age of forty-five. But for the rest of us the lessons are clear— never overplay. Be unselfish in your playing and compliment the band; you are the engine of each song, so drive that train; and always remember that you're not a machine, so swing it!

Curt Weiss *is the author of* Stranded In The Jungle: Jerry Nolan's Wild Ride. *Using the stage name Lewis King, he drummed for Beat Rodeo, Elliott Murphy, and The Rockats. He has spent close to thirty years working in TV production, helping manage several PBS documentaries including* The ACLU: A History *and* Vaudeville *for American Masters.*

YOU'RE ONLY AS GOOD AS YOUR DRUMMER

By John Robb

Y OU'RE ONLY AS GOOD as your drummer."
Those wise words are from punk rock warlord Joe Strummer talking about Clash drummer, Topper Headon, in the 2000 documentary *The Clash:Westway to the World*. Once the drummer had been kicked out of the band in May 1982 because of his escalating drug problems, they started the downward spiral that saw them fall apart shortly afterward. Years later, Strummer recognized this and by extension just how key so many of the drummers in that period were to their bands.

Topper was one of the leading drummers of the punk era, an awesome talent whose polyrhythmic possibilities made the Clash such a huge success and capable of the cross-genre styles that became their trademark. Without the drummer, their adventures into dub, funk, soul, rockabilly, and hip hop would have been nowhere near as convincing. His tight snare rolls are part of his signature sound, and he also wrote the band's biggest hit, "Rock the Casbah."

The drummer is the key to every band and their rhythms are at the core of their music era. Every generation gets to deal with its own blues, with its own rhythm—whether it's the pounding rush of fifties rock and roll, the Black music-influenced Cavern stomp of the Beatles, the sixties British post-beat innovation, the intricate mind melting pattern of the hippies and prog, the juggernaut post-industrial power of John Bonham, the rising four-to-the-floor of disco, or the almost military-staccato rush of punk rock drumming.

Much has been written about the music style, politics, and attitude of late-seventies bands, but interestingly little gets said about the drumming. The machine gun guitars and guttural vocals are endlessly detailed, but this was also an era when there were many great drummers creating their own beat narrative. Punk's attempts to deconstruct rock-and-roll and trad-rock rhythm to find a new style and language of its own is one of the keys to the form. This journey continued on into post punk with the drummers leading this escape from the past.

Punk was awkward, deliberately so. Many of the initial bands were trying to create a new musical language far away from the suffocating avalanche of rock and roll. The blues-fused rock had dominated the airwaves and the discourse for a couple of decades, but the newer British bands, coming through in 1976, were trying to find their own language, energies, and rhythms. This put many of the new generation of drummers into a unique position of creating a new rhythmic language that was post rock and roll while embracing disco, tribal patterns, and, more importantly, the space and possibility of dub into their sound and playing.

A key, if lesser known, example would be the Slits. The revolutionary punk inner circle band were fronted by explosive fourteen-year-old singer Ari Up, whose mother Nora would marry John Lydon. Ari Up was a precocious wild child who loved the space of dub and the energy and potential of punk. She wanted a band that played feminine rhythms at a punky reggae party. Her first drummer, Palmolive, played powerful, simplistic beats and wrote many of the band's defining early songs. After she had left, the second phase of the band saw Ari Up's vision of feminine rhythms ironically come to fruition with a male drummer from St. Helens near Liverpool called Budgie now behind the kit. His empathy, sensitivity, and polyrhythmic style was explored in his powerful and urgent playing that fused the space of dub with the four-on-the-floor kick drum borrowed from disco and an off-kilter pattern play that would be a key influence on post punk. Budgie would soon go on to join Siouxsie and the Banshees and bring his signature style into that band's darker vision.

Punk was an opportunity for these new young drummers to break down the clichés. The fabric had been torn and, before it became a form of music, anything went. Punk bands were often formed as an idea and not as a collection of musicians. They had manifestos and ideas of what they could and what they could not do. Often it was more about what you were not than what you were—like with Siouxsie dictating that she didn't want a drummer using cymbals in their early days, deliberating pushing the band's brilliant young drummer Kenny Morris toward a starker pounding style. He played on the band's first two albums with a razor-tight style that was often built around tribal toms that helped to give the band a unique edge. One of the great unsung heroes of the period, Morris left behind a distinctive style that has been imitated endlessly as punk morphed into post punk.

DIY was one of the pillars of punk rock. Anyone could do it. This was key to the inventiveness as it meant you made your own rules and your own musical style. Post-punk DIY was already influenced by these ideas and ideals that were counterpointed by the fact that many of the first wave of British punk bands were already good and groundbreaking players who were reinventing rock and roll very quickly. Like many musicians of the time, it was about finding your own style and honing that down to perfection. Sometimes it was about instinct and creative intensity.

In Manchester in late 1976, a sixteen-year-old John Maher joined the only local punk band, Buzzcocks, and learned to play in four weeks flat before recording the band's first release, the 4-track, game-changing *Spiral Scratch* EP. It was a remarkable achievement and so typical of the speed of the time. Released in January 1977, *Spiral Scratch* was the first independent release of the punk period and saw Buzzcocks take punk out of the London inner circle and into Manchester and the rest of the world. The pithy, buzz saw guitar-driven songs were held together by the hyper-kinetic drum patterns of the gangling young drummer who stepped up to the plate very early in his career.

Maher was a natural, but also brought something different to the table. His drums were key to Buzzcocks and, through the band's three punk-era albums, were astonishing in their rhythmic variety and power, all while also unconsciously creating a template for the post-punk period with every instrument playing lead and not a backup.

Maher rarely settled on the trad 4/4 and utilized the whole kit in brilliant patterns that could be quite complex but danceable. They were always punchy and almost always with a powerful melody of their own, if such a thing is possible on drums. Some tracks, like "Moving Away from the Pulsebeat," use the drums as the lead instrument for key chunks of the song with a pattern that you could almost sing in your head.

Every punk band was driven by a distinctive, powerful, and lyrical drummer—a combination of the explosive energy of youth and a determination to make your own mark in what was then perceived to be a very short-lived musical form. This drove young drummers like Rat Scabies from the Damned.

Scabies' explosive drumming on the Damned's 1976 debut single "New Rose" and the *Damned Damned Damned* album marked him out quickly. He could have been the Keith Moon of his generation, but like everything else about this classic band, his career staggered in stops and starts. On the group's debut album, though, his sheer visceral power is still quite shocking to this day. The pounding tom-toms of "New Rose" are an avalanche of energy, and his drumming across the whole album sounds enormous. It's incredible to anyone who ever visited the tiny (and now demolished) Pathway Studios in Camden, where the album was recorded, that something so visceral and loud could have been recorded in a space the size of a tiny front room. It was that combination between Scabies' wild and feral power and album producer Nick Lowe's great use of compression that created some of the most thrilling drum sounds ever committed to vinyl.

The Damned were one of the original three British punk bands—the triumvirate of groups who coalesced in London in late 1975 through 1976. The alpha groups of the musical revolution each had their own distinct style and sound. The instigators, of course, were the Sex Pistols, and their drummer Paul Cook is one of the great British drummers. His style is so distinctive that you can immediately recognize his playing, either with the Sex Pistols or, later on, with Edwyn Collins or Vic Godard. It's easy to overlook the sheer musicality of the band, but the Sex Pistols were far more than a wonderful media hype and story while dressed to the nines in super sharp punk duds. Without their musical engine room, they would not have worked. Without the hype, they would still have made an impression but Paul Cook's drums were a key part of this.

Unlike the other two bands in the big three, the Clash were not initially built upon the bedrock of a great drummer. For the first part of their career, the core three piece of the famously charismatic frontline were always seeking a permanent sticksman. A whole procession of drummers went through their Rehearsal Rehearsals space in Camden Town as the band tried to find someone who looked and sounded right.

For their iconic March 1977 debut album, they used Terry Chimes as their drummer. Rechristened Tory Crimes on the album cover because he once joked that he would like to have a sports car as a reward for being in the band, his almost out of breath, short, sharp shocks of drumming suited the band's initial punk phase. This style would become a template for many of the second-wave punk bands who sped up his rhythmic flurries and almost military rolls into a style of their own before it hit maximum velocity with the D-beat style of hardcore punk pioneered by Discharge.

The songs on the Clash's debut album were missives and snapshots of London street life at the time, an amphetamine psychosis of a then-gloomy, post-industrial, post-war decaying Victorian City that was a million miles away from its pre-Corvid peak. With a musician like Mick Jones in the band constantly curious about other styles of music, the Clash were never going to be a static affair. To realize that ambition, they needed a new drummer, bringing in Topper Headon.

He was nicknamed "Topper" by bassist Paul Simonon after cartoon character Mickey the Monkey from *The Topper* comic. Fascinated with Bruce Lee and Jeet Kune Do, Topper was a jobbing drummer who had claimed to have played with the Temptations and many other bands. Initially not from the punk world, he learned his chops on the pick-up band circuit, and his huge portfolio of styles and ability would revolutionize the Clash. It gave them the capability to stretch out through a myriad of musical forms of music beyond punk and further into the dub and reggae that they had already toyed with on their cover of Junior Murvin's "Police and Thieves" on their debut album. With Topper behind the kit, they could go deeper into dub and reggae and then through the disco, funk, and soul that would become key to the band's development. It was all fully captured on their game-changing late 1979 third album, *London Calling*.

Around the same time, Mick Jones' best buddy Tony James had formed his own, poppier punk band with Billy Idol on vocals called Generation X. Yet another band whose musical capabilities were far ahead of their youthful energy, the band featured Mark Laff on drums. The then twenty-year-old drummer was another stand out player in the classic year of 1977.

The eternal misfits of the scene were the Stranglers. They were certainly not part of the inner circle, but with a genuine whiff of cordite danger, malevolence, and a unique sound driven by the late Dave Greenfield's funereal, lysergic keyboards and JJ Burnel's stunning lead black belt bass—and with a talent for writing infernally catchy and decadently dangerous songs—the band were embraced by the punk generation teenagers who recognized the outlaw vibe of the group. The band's bedrock was provided by Jet Black who, at thirty-nine, was already the old man in a younger punk world. He played that vintage to his advantage, though, with a box of rhythmic tricks that dated back to his jazz roots in the fifties. A big burly man, he could hit the drums hard but always played with an intelligence and an ear for unique drum patterns. This scope of styles was explored as the band opened up their sound to off-kilter rhythms like the 13/8 on the band's biggest hit, "Golden Brown," the 6/8 of "Princess of the Streets"—one of the key tracks of the band's astonishing debut—or the utterly distinctive 9/4 of 1977's "Peasant in the Big Shitty," and the bizarre complexities of 1979's "Genetix." Perhaps the first example of a punk period band who were playing all the instruments as lead, the Stranglers were well placed to pull this off with their audacious musical capabilities.

Another drummer who toyed with the dislocation of rhythm was Stephen Morris of Joy Division. He was the last to join the iconic Manchester band, but his innate love of mid-seventies German Krautrock and its Motorik beat saw him up for deconstructing the band's rhythms. The debut Joy Division album is a testament to this. To this day, the Martin Hannett production sounds like something from the future and Morris's drums were the most treated part of the revolutionary sound mix. Hannett's love of gates and the harmonizers with the ever-changing reverbs—many of which he had invented himself—made the drums sound off kilter, ghostly, and ethereal. Yet the songs were still danceable with a nod to the influential incoming disco scene and the added new tech of Syndrum. This mix of post-punk, disco, and tech can also be heard in other groundbreaking drummers of the period like Kevin Haskins from Bauhaus.

The apocryphal story of Hannett making Morris play his drum patterns one part of the drum kit at a time sums up the punk attitude of breaking boundaries and clichés that was so key at the time. The genius of course was that Morris could somehow make whatever wild idea was thrown at him by the maverick producer sound like a drum pattern no matter what the wild-eyed Hannett wanted.

With a flux of new influences from dub to disco to funk, the early post-punk period saw a lot of other fascinating rhythmic experiments thrown into its soup of ideas. In 1980, the ever-inquisitive new generation of musicians were constantly looking beyond rock for new shapes and patterns and, in interest of other cultures, saw so-called tribal rhythms added to the mix. There had been hints of this even in the earliest days of punk's Big Bang with Siouxsie and the Banshees first drummer, Kenny Morris.

The exotic and thrilling power of tribal rhythms suited punk. The fusing of the sound and styles from all over the world was easy to assimilate in the scene's bricolage mindset. Adam and the Ants' young drummer, Dave Barbe (a.k.a. Barbarossa), had already played a blinder on the band's 1978 debut album, *Dirk Wears White Sox*. He was still the band's drummer when the front man brought in Malcolm McLaren to give his advice on how to break out of monochromatic cult status. The wily manager gave the band an eclectic cassette of music that included crooners, Egyptian wedding music, and Burundi drumming. Toying with the distinctive pounding patterns, the band changed direction but after two rehearsals they split from their charismatic singer, lured away by McLaren to form Bow Wow Wow and continue these new sound experiments with singer Annabella Lwin.

Adam Ant dusted himself down, rising up to become the biggest star in the UK in 1981 with his *Kings of the Wild Frontier* album that melded glam rock guitars, feedback, cinematic soundscapes, and lots of wild and thrilling Burundi drums. It is one of the most original art rock albums, but also dared push pop to its limits. The added triumphant rumble of the two drummers, Chris Thomas and Terry Lee Miall, was the key signature of the sound and still sounds startlingly original to this day.

The tribal style was now everywhere in that early eighties post-punk period. Already immersed in the rhythms of funk and dub meshed with a ferocious intensity, Killing Joke experimented with their version of it. Their drummer Paul Ferguson delivered his own distinctive take on the tribal style with powerful tom-toms and imaginative playing allied to an astonishing power.

Even Public Image Limited's fourth album, *The Flowers of Romance*, saw a really sparse, astonishingly claustrophobic, and powerful take on tribal beats by drummer Martin Atkins. Meanwhile the Fall had a dabble with drummer Karl Burns, adding to their Motorik-infused armory and at one point, during their classic *Hex Induction Hour* period, having two drummers with a youthful Paul Hanley counterpointing Burns' angular workouts.

These new rhythms were everywhere. Crass crisscrossed classical music, free jazz, and military drumming in the anarchic punk rushes. There was the minimalism of Robert Gotobed's drums in Wire, and the powerful and always well thought out drumming of Terry Chambers in XTC, whose patterns mixed a sparse power with African counter rhythms, especially on the bands *English Settlement* album where producer Hugh Padgham further added the live ambience that he had been playing with on the drums to help create the distinctive and powerful sound.

Everywhere you listened in that period bands were playing with the form. Punk drummers were all looking for their own identity. It was an arms race in originality with stunning results. Very few musical waves have seen such intense competition to create something new and the drums were at the forefront in this creative rush.

John Robb *is a many-faceted creature of punk rock. Bassist and singer for post-punk mainstays The Membranes, author, journalist, DJ, publisher, and talking head, he's all these things and more. John runs the leading music and culture website Louder Than War. He also runs a music and books festival called Louderthanwar and is a political campaigner who chairs committees in Parliament and is an in demand speaker with his spoken word show spawned by the success of his talks of TEDx on punk, zen and the universe and also for his talks of veganism and punk rock called, "The world accruing to John Robb." He also tours the world.*

TOP FIVE FAVORITE PUNK DRUMMERS

By Hudley Flipside

IN 1978, I WAS A trained graphic artist, which means I used an X-Acto knife and could draw a straight line. I plunged into the world of Los Angeles punk rock as a nobody punk among nobody punks. Yet I created a name for myself, HUD or Hudley Flipside. *Los Angeles Flipside Fanzine* soon seized me. I fell in love and quickly became a coeditor and publisher for ten years. *Flipside Fanzine* met lots of bands along its journey. Punk is all about experience, friendship, and a song…one song to the next kept me fucking addicted. I currently own a company, The Seminary of Praying Mantis Publishing, that recently published two paperback books relating to punk rock—*Los Angeles Flipside Fanzine # 54 Ten Year Anniversary Issue* (replica) and its side kick, *My Punkalullaby.*

Ivor Hay
The Saints

In any image of the original members of the Saints (1973–1978), you will see Ivor Hay dressed in dark clothing. He is tall, thin, has short blond hair, and often wears dark sunglasses. The original incognito guy, a punk drumming saint found about town, in a bar, or a dark alley. "One Way Street" is the second song off the

Saints' debut album. Ed Kuepper starts with lead guitar before Hay explodes in with his unique pulsation. A call for the underground music to begin. The original drum beat of punk rock. My only current addiction is this band.

Scott Miller
Agent Orange

This three-piece surf-punk band shines bright. Hearing the original trio of Steve Soto on bass, Scott Miller on drums, and the infamous Mike Palm on guitar together is great. The Posh Boy Records recording (1979) of the song "Bloodstains" is a winner punk anthem. Happy-beat Scott stuck with the band and was always a joy to talk to. Agent Orange skates on the cover of *Los Angeles Flipside Fanzine* #42. Scott also is viewed pouring a drink over his head. One of the best drummers and characters to send a throbbing rhythm down my spine.

Lucky Lehrer
Circle Jerks

Many bands tumbled in the back door of Posh Boy Records to get their careers going; Circle Jerks is one of those bands. They were out-of-control good. Lucky is a trained jazz drummer who was a smartass. The sixth track, "Wasted," off the *Group Sex* album has Lucky's fast drum roll confidence. I remember in a *Flipside Fanzine* interview with Circle Jerks, Lucky confronted me, saying that not voting in presidential elections is pathetic. I gave him the empty punk reason for not voting. He told me most punks think that way and it is wrong. Got me thinking about politics differently. He is smart, fun, and a thrill to hang out with.

Reed Mullin
Corrosion of Conformity

Of the many bands that toured through Los Angeles in the 1980s, COC is one that rings loudly in my memory. They started the fast-hardcore sound or, as we knew it, thrash bands. Reed was active in the punk scene and seemed to know all the punk hubs. He shared and bootlegged music cassettes. He made me, with much opposition, listen to a cassette tape of a nobody metal band named Metallica. An intense and gut-wrenching drummer boy. One of my favorite Reed drum songs is "13 Angels." Slower than I remember him drumming, yet older and wiser. Rest in peace, sweet prince.

Scott Preece
GBH

When Charged GBH first hit the punk scene in the early 1980s, I knew the band's original drummer, Wilf. Then, a few years later, Scott Preece joined the band. Finally, I got to see the song "Lycanthropy" live, a number off their debut album *Leather, Bristle, Studs, and Acne* (1981). I'd waited years to hear it live. My youngest son drums. He told me that Scott sounds like drums on steroids. The second time I casually met Scott was at the Rainbow Bar and Grill on the Sunset Strip before a show. I sat next to him drinking a pint of beer. Before I left, I told him how much his style of drumming improved the band. He was surprised I knew who he was. When it comes to GBH, I know who is drumming with bass player Ross Lomas and Jock Blyth on guitar. The best damn punk sound in the universe.

Hudley Flipside *is the publisher of the memoir* My Punkalullaby *and* Los Angeles Flipside Fanzine # 54 Ten-Year Anniversary *(Replica). Hudley Flipside is the pen name of Holly Cornell, owner of The Seminary of Praying Mantis Publishing, she co-owned and edited punk fanzine* Los Angeles Flipside Fanzine *from 1979–1989.*

DRUMS>VIOLINS

By Bon Von Wheelie

I WAS TEN YEARS older than the guys in my band and one of
them was my brother.

I should back up a bit. I'm the female drummer in the band
Girl Trouble. We've been together for thirty-six years, and when
I was a kid in the sixties, I never thought I'd ever play drums or
any musical instrument for that matter. The school system didn't
offer drum lessons to girls in 1963. We got violin. That was it.

I remember walking by all the boys tapping out rhythms on
those little practice pads. I was stuck with a violin that looked
damn cool but sounded like shit when I played it. I just could
not get into this instrument. The music didn't move me, and
practicing seemed like torture, not only for me but I'm sure for
my family who had to endure it. I took lessons for a year and
was about the worst in the class. Convinced I wasn't musically
inclined, I dropped out before our first official "concert."

That didn't mean I wasn't soaking up music. I couldn't get
enough of the rhythm and blues records I heard on the radio.
And then the world changed immediately when the Beatles
showed up (along with my little brother Bill who was born on the
second Sunday the Beatles appeared on *The Ed Sullivan Show*).
They lead the way for the British Invasion. And the way those

drummers, especially Ringo Starr and Charlie Watts, held down the whole thing just by pumping out a solid beat made me crazy. Local groups like the Sonics and the Wailers, and bands like Tiny Tony and the Statics and Jimmy Hanna and the Dynamics, were on my constant playlist. I was too young to go see them perform, but I wasn't too young to have my ear glued to our old radio. I even remember getting some old knitting needles to see if I could tap out a beat to the Rolling Stones' "Satisfaction."

Rock and roll was an important part of my life, even if I wasn't playing it. I went to every concert I could back in my "hippie" days, and I really did learn how bands put on a show. Ike & Tina Turner, B. B. King, the Who, Jimi Hendrix, Buddy Miles Express, Sly and the Family Stone—that was better schooling than I ever had with that damn violin. At the same time, I was going to dances at the Crescent Ballroom and the BreakThru (Red Carpet) in Tacoma, Washington, to see local groups. But as things went, the giant arena show replaced all those medium/small events that had all the energy. I loved the music, but the huge shows seemed so impersonal. I lost interest in going to the "EnormoDome" with 50,000 other people to see a band that looked like ants.

By this time, my little brother Bill suddenly discovered all my old records. He started listening to all those amazing bands that I grew up with. I thought that was great. At least he could grow up with the classics, even though I was a little disappointed that he probably would never know the excitement of seeing bands up close like I had.

Bill became a teenager and punk rock hit our house. He brought home Ramones, B-52s, and Sex Pistols records, and it was easy for me to immediately love them. Live music was vital again. You could go to small/medium sized venues to see all the new bands we had been listening to. The energy was absolutely unbelievable. Bill and his friends allowed me to tag along to see all the groups coming through Seattle. Music was really exciting again.

These kids were always trying to form bands, but nobody ever had drums. Guitars were easier to come by. While they were okay with me tagging along for shows, I'm not sure I was exactly the type of person they wanted to join a band. But Bill started learning guitar to all the records he had, and I decided that I'd get a cheap drum set. I went to the Sears Surplus Store and picked out a beaut for seventy-five bucks. There was no brand name, and the bass drum was only about twenty inches. Lots of real drummers told me it was cute. I just practiced to records by myself and then Bill (a.k.a. Kahuna) decided that maybe he could use a timekeeper. That's how we started, learning together. Before we knew it, Bill's best school friend, Dale Phillips, came by to play bass. We coaxed a good friend Kurt P. Kendall—who was the life of every party—to sing with us.

This is the same time we discovered the Cramps and the Gun Club. I have to say that was an inspiration, Nick Knox of the Cramps was picking up where Ringo and Charlie had started. I've never wanted to play much more than a solid beat. I can appreciate the fancy guys (Keith Moon, etc.), but it's always just been the raw beat that gets me going. Nick Knox had it in spades and that style worked out with our band Girl Trouble.

I finally ditched the Sears drum set for a Ludwig 1965. The guy at the store made me promise that I wouldn't bring it back. He figured it was just a fluke, that a twenty-eight-year-old woman would quickly decide drumming wasn't for her. I knew what he meant. Not that many women my age were playing drums in teenage bands.

I eventually had to retire the Ludwig kit because it was getting too beat up in the van without cases. I now have a really great standard Gretsch drum set that I've been playing for the last fifteen years. I still play just like I started out—the beat. I think I'm good at that. That's what it's all about for me, and I'm glad I found something other than the violin.

Bon Von Wheelie *was born in Tacoma, Washington, and started drumming at age thirty and formed a band with her little brother and his friends. That band, Girl Trouble, has been together since 1984 and is still active to this day. They've toured US, Canada, and Europe; released records on many PNW independent labels; and published their own fanzine* Wig Out! *The documentary* Strictly Sacred: The Story of Girl Trouble *debuted at the Seattle International Film Festival in 2014.*

JOEY SHITHEAD ON CHUCK BISCUITS

Interviewed by S. W. Lauden

Singer/guitarist Joey "Shithead" Keithley formed the legendary Canadian punk band D.O.A. in 1978. That original line up featured a teenage drummer named Charles Montgomery who became a legend under his stage name, Chuck Biscuits. Although D.O.A. continues to tour and record forty years later, the band only released two full-length albums with Biscuits, *Something Better Change* and *Hardcore 81*. It was still the dawn of West Coast hardcore when he developed a signature style that many fans and musicians still consider the template for hardcore drumming. Biscuits left D.O.A. before the band's third album, *War on 45*, and went on to play with everybody from Black Flag and Circle Jerks to Danzig and Social Distortion.

Can you tell me how D.O.A. formed?

I was in a band called the Skulls from Vancouver. The drummer in the that band was Dimwit [Ken Montgomery]. The Skulls broke up, so I ran an ad in the local paper looking for "a drummer to start a punk band." I heard that Dimwit's younger brother Chuck [Charles Montgomery] wanted to try out, and he was like fifteen at the time. So, we tried him out and thought "wow, this guy's great—tons of potential." And there was Randy Rampage

[Randall Archibald] who was a decent drummer, but I thought I could probably teach him how to play bass. I started out as a drummer too from the time I was eleven until I was eighteen. So, D.O.A. was a band made up of three drummers, which I think is obvious on the first couple albums because it's rhythmically forceful. Clearly Chuck was the best of the three.

What was your impression of Chuck as a drummer when D.O.A. first started?

Chuck was really quick. I would consider Chuck and his brother Dimwit to be two of the greatest drummers to come out of Canada, and I'm not just talking about punk drummers. Dimwit was more of a heavy hitter, a heavy rock drummer like John Bonham. But Chuck was really quick with those fast rolls and, back in the day, people used to marvel at him. I still marvel at how good he was at that age.

Dimwit used to have a garage off his house where we'd jam with Wimpy [Brian Roy Goble] and Gerry Hannah from the Subhumans. We all lived three blocks from each other, so we'd jam in Dimwit's garage. When Chuck was thirteen, he'd drum along with us on the bongos. That's where he got his start. Little did we know he was going to turn into a punk rock phenom. A lot of great drummers have come out of punk rock, but Chuck's reputation is well-deserved.

Is there an interesting backstory to your stage names?

Dimwit gave me my nickname. We were going to start a punk band called Joey Shithead and the Marching Morons. Well, the "Marching Morons" never happened, but I took "Shithead." And Randy's last name was Archibald and I thought "you can't be in a punk band with that last name," so he became Randy Rampage. And Charles was "Upchuck Biscuits" at first. Then it just got chopped to "Chuck Biscuits," but I can't remember who came up with the name. It might have been Chuck himself, but I don't remember anymore. That was part of the charm of D.O.A., you had Rampage, Biscuits, and Shithead.

Something Better Change *is a fantastic debut album. Listening back forty years later, I'm struck by the stylistic similarities to first-wave British punk bands. Who were some of D.O.A.'s main influences back then?*

We all grew up listening to rock music because punk rock hadn't come along. So D.O.A. has this backbeat to it that was originally rock and roll, but obviously we sped it up a whole bunch. I saw the Ramones the first time they came to Vancouver in the summer of 1977, so they were an influence for sure. Later on, we listened to the Clash a lot, and I don't think it's any secret that D.O.A. got some inspiration from the Clash, politically and musically. We were big fans.

But it was still at the end of the seventies rock era. The big bands like the Who, Led Zeppelin, Deep Purple—that was the kind of stuff that me and Randy listened to in high school. Black Sabbath, of course. So, when we started out recording, Chuck would sometimes ask what he should play and we would say "What would Keith Moon would do?" That was kind of the key, because Moon was a wild man. Chuck took that to heart and was kind of a wild man on the drums, too.

His drumming takes a huge leap forward on your second album,* Hardcore 81. *In my mind, that's the album that sets the template for a lot of hardcore drumming. What changed?

Something Better Change came out in May or June of 1980. We had done a little bit of touring, but at that point we were driving down to California every four weeks, playing five shows, and driving back. Then we started doing full on tours, just traveling all the time. We were pretty committed. We took out a loan on a van, so all the money went into paying for the van and gas, which is a pretty typical story.

So, it was all that touring. Chuck and Randy were at their peak. They just synched up really well as a rhythm section back then. Pretty much all the songs on *Something Better Change* and *Hardcore 81* were on our set list starting in 1979. When you keep playing the same songs over and over again, they become fine-tuned. Our manager at the time thought the first record should have a few more melodic songs, that's where you got "2 + 2" and "New Age" and songs like that. The songs on *Hardcore 81* were kind of the leftovers, so that album had a faster clip.

That was during the transition from the Sex Pistols and the Clash era into bands like Bad Brains and Dead Kennedys, more of a hardcore approach—although it wasn't called that yet—that sounded less like Britain and New York. We thought it sounded like the West Coast, even though there were other hardcore scenes in New York, Boston, and Washington, DC. We needed our own sound and we thought that was bands like D.O.A., Black Flag, and Circle Jerks, so we just called it "hardcore." We wanted it faster, louder, and meaner.

Was Chuck involved at all with your third album, War on 45?

We were doing demos for *War on 45* in March of 1982. At that point Randy had left the band, so Chuck's older brother Dimwit became the bass player. He was a great drummer and had a mean sense of rhythm (rest his soul, since he's not with us anymore), but it was a weird scenario for Chuck to have his older brother looking over his shoulder. Before that nobody ever told Chuck what to do with his drumming, but Dimwit was well-qualified to critique him. So, one day we're rehearsing songs for *War on 45* and we're playing a reggae song called "War in the East." Chuck was playing a lot of fills and Dimwit told him not to. Chuck had been in the band since the beginning, but here comes his older brother telling him what to do. Finally, Chuck said "Fuck you guys, I quit."

It was the end of an era and sadly we never played another note of music together again. Obviously, Chuck went on to play with a bunch of phenomenal bands like Black Flag, Circle Jerks, Social Distortion, and Danzig. That's a pretty sterling track record.

What are a few of your favorite D.O.A. tracks with Chuck Biscuits on drums?

The one that kills every drummer who has been in D.O.A. since Chuck left is the end of "Slumlord." Those fast rolls are hard to do, especially sustained over eight bars or sixteen bars. Other songs on *Hardcore 81* that stand out are "Unknown" and "D.O.A." is really great. "Waiting For You" is crazy, sort of the genesis of hardcore for D.O.A. And from the first record "New Age," "The Enemy," and "World War III" stand out. Chuck was an excellent songwriter, too. There were other bandmembers I wrote with, but not as much as Chuck. It was an honor to play with him.

THE NIGHTMARE CONTINUES: DECONSTRUCTING THE D-BEAT

By Matt Diehl

Play to this.
It's a bit quick, Tezz.
Yeah? So what?
—Tezz Roberts, *But After the Gig...*

I F PUNK ROCK HAS an equivalent to the Bo Diddley beat, it can only be the D-beat. It's arguably the most influential rhythmic figure to come out of all of punk—even more international in its reach, perhaps, than its American cousin, US hardcore's "forbidden beat."

"[D-beat] is not only a recognized musical style, but a very specific drum rhythm—much in the same way, say, as samba to Latin music or one drop is to reggae," notes veteran punk drummer Spike T. Smith (who's played with the Damned, Morrissey, New York Dolls, Killing Joke, and D-beat legends Sacrilege, among others) in his short, sharp YouTube documentary on the subject, *The Birth of the D-Beat...Punk Meets Hardcore.* "It existed a long time before any punk band was putting it to good use, that's for sure," Smith adds, noting similar rhythms could be found in everything from the Velvet Underground to various genres of Latin music.

The forbidden beat and the D-beat were certainly the most fashionable rhythmic choices when it came to eighties punk's attempts to set land speed records. The former was primarily the province of acts like Minor Threat—a caffeinated, amateurish 4/4 thump with a distinct oompah vibe. The D-beat, meanwhile, began via the trademark tattoo popularized by the most iconic band of UK punk's second wave, Discharge.

Also typically rendered in 4/4, Discharge's D-beat added Burundi-influenced toms and syncopated rhythmic nuances arriving at unexpected times in the musical measures—creating its signature galloping pocket in the process. While sounding equally as extreme and intense as the forbidden beat, these choices made the D-beat a more open and musical framework for Discharge to sandwich its jackhammer unison riffage into, all without disturbing its relentless forward assault. There was air for the bombs to pass through before they exploded unexpectedly.

"That's what's distinctive, *innit*—the hand is following the foot, while the quarter note played by the right hand smooths it out," Spike Smith muses in *The Birth of the D-Beat*. D-beat's Wikipedia page posits that there are three versions of the D-beat, all variations on a basic formula. The Discharge-style D-beat came from the band's visionary cofounder and second drummer Tezz Roberts on the title track of its first official release, the groundbreaking *Realities of War* EP. (It should be noted, I interviewed Tezz in a kind of meta fashion for this essay: essentially, I would ask him questions via Facebook messenger, and he would respond in an iconoclastically post-Internet manner by sending links to YouTube videos—some relating to the question, others not. Truth be told, it was still a fascinating, illuminating exchange!)

In Tezz's playing on Discharge's earliest D-beat classics— and that of his successors in Discharge, first Dave "Bambi"

Ellesmere (also of D-beat band the Varukers) and then Garry Maloney, both brilliant musicians—the ride cymbals, crashes, and floor toms alternate abruptly for variety, all while striving for maximum impact by staying tautly within the parameters of Tezz's effectively brutalist, minimalist template. The other trick to D-beat was that it sounded deceptively simple to play, inspiring endless imitators. In actual practice, however, it proved incredibly challenging to pull off—due to both the sheer physical exertion required to maintain it, as well as the necessity to reduce its more complex counts to muscle memory.

"You can count the quarter notes as eighth notes in two-measure phrasing—which is easier when you're talking about playing really fast tempos," explains veteran punk drummer Adam Zuckert, who's served as sticksman for Discharge-influenced bands Final Conflict and F-Minus. "It's 'one *and* two *and* three *and* four' versus one-two-three-four. The D-beat's syncopated kick on the up 'and' notes creates a different feel than everything being on the down beats in the 'forbidden beat.' Add in variations of the kick patterns and two measure phrasings, and you can see there's actually a lot of creativity and differentiation to be had."

Vastly influential, the D-beat would go on to transcend its rhythmic origins, inspiring various related splinterings of Discharge's punk aesthetic. While crust and anarcho-punk to street punk were predictable outgrowths of the D-beat sound, at the same time, it drew adopters even from outside punk's stylistically stratified boundaries. As such, while Discharge would initially be pigeonholed as thrash amidst the various stylist punk subdivisions, D-beat would eventually be considered a genre unto itself—taking its name, even, from its rhythmic foundation. Numerous D-beat bands, in fact, affix "Dis" as the prefix in their moniker (Disfear, Disclose, Dishammer, et al.) to pledge allegiance to their forefathers.

And well after. Indeed, one doesn't necessarily need to be a punk enthusiast to have experienced the D-beat; it's genetically present in nearly all contemporary popular music that aspires to take music to its loudest, fastest, most aggressive extreme. In a sort of chicken-and-egg give and take, the D-beat has proven an indisputable part of contemporary heavy metal's DNA for the past four decades—extending its crusty tentacles into the varietals of thrash, crossover, doom, death, powerviolence, sludge, and even Scandinavian melodic power metal. Heavy titans ranging from Metallica, Anthrax, and Sepultura to Napalm Death, Machine Head, and At the Gates have covered Discharge songs. D-beat's influence, meanwhile, proves omnipresent in bands spanning various extremes of heaviness, from Neurosis and Corrosion of Conformity to Bathory, Helmet, and Slayer. Celtic Frost cofounder Tom G. Warrior, in fact, considers Discharge's influence to have inspired a "revolution" in heavy metal's sonic aesthetics.

"When I heard the first two Discharge records, I was blown away," Warrior told *Decibel*'s J. Bennet. "I was just starting to play an instrument and I had no idea you could go so far. And to me, they were unlike other punk bands—they sounded more like metal."

And there was a reason for that. D-beat's viral capacity for cross-species transmission makes sense considering metal served as a crucial element of its definitive formation. Discharge proved the perfect crucible to bring together all its molecular elements in what was clearly a zeitgeist moment in the rhythmic spectrum.

Punk, however, would provide D-beat's gateway drug into notoriety. The first recorded examples of the D-beat came from England punk originators the Buzzcocks via the band's stone-classic songs "You Tear Me Up" and "Everybody's Happy Nowadays." In fact, in *The Birth of the D-Beat*, Buzzcocks drummer John Maher recalls lurching into the rhythm on "You Tear Me Up" as his first order of business in his debut rehearsal with the band in 1976. As such, that defining moment proved a happy-accident meeting of amateurism, deconstruction, and innovation for the then-seventeen-year-old novice with a crap Sonor Swinger drum kit.

"I remember the very first time I played it, I went 'round to Howard's basement flat," Maher says. "It was literally being thrown into the deep end: 'We've got this song, it goes like this... one-two-three-four!'" As for the related thump in "Everybody's Happy Nowadays," Maher remembers it came about by turning a mistake into a style choice. "The hi-hat needed to be a steady thing—and I couldn't do it!" he says. "Two years later, I would've been able to. But it worked out for the best!"

"You Tear Me Up" first appeared on 1978's *Time's Up* bootleg, capturing the band's first demo session, recorded in October 1976 at Revolution Studios in suburban Manchester; "Everybody's Happy Nowadays," meanwhile, appeared as the A-side of a non-album single release in 1979. Maher's interpretation of this beat proved the essence of punk—the rhythm embodied a different kind of rhythmic tension, utterly and thrillingly distinct from the prog and hard rock stylings of the day. Seemingly tossed off, simultaneously swinging and metronomic in its violently shifting dynamics, Maher's nascent D-beat was the human musical approximation of an industrial accident—a machine that has gone off its gears and could fall apart at any time. And in the best punk tradition, it sounded effortless and democratic—its childlike pulse intelligently designed to sound so that seemingly anyone could play it.

The D-beat as we think of it today evolved out of what's become known as "UK82"—the punk movement and sound that evolved a half decade after punk entered England's collective consciousness. In that five-year span, punk evolved sonically and aesthetically, as things do, but it's especially important in a genre iconoclastically devoted to never being stuck long in any conventional musical space. The Clash and Sex Pistols distinguished themselves from the symphonic ambitions, cosmic obsessions, and virtuoso guitar solos of Pink Floyd and Queen by combining the stripped-down instrumentation and brisk tempos of fifties rock, sixties garage, and the first Ramones albums— marrying that alarming cacophony to a bird's eye view of society descending into urban-dystopian Thatcherism.

Bands were starting to take that approach to greater extremes, however, even in the first wave. Tempos started inching up faster and faster, even among the genre's originators. Take *It's Alive* by the Ramones, a double-LP set capturing one of the band's most significant gigs impacting the original UK punk scene, for example. The live recording vividly captures the OG New York punks' blazing set at London's famed Rainbow Theatre on New Year's Eve 1977. Attended by prominent local punk cognoscenti, the Ramones (powered by original drummer Tommy Ramone) played that night with even greater energy, momentum, and wildness than on their first three albums. The visceral excitement of their barrage, in fact, drove audience members to tear their seats off the floor and hurl them at the stage!

An early US tour of the Damned in 1979 also proved similarly inspiring. Future "forbidden beat" hardcore progenitors like Ian MacKaye and Henry Rollins were left dazed by the intense performances of the first English punk group to have a commercial release. At the Damned's Washington, DC, stop, MacKaye noted that the band, propelled by drummer Rat Scabies, seemed to triple the tempos established on the band's already propulsive studio recordings; meanwhile, the show's dazzling opening act, Bad Brains (with bravura drummer Earl Hudson behind the kit) were also taking punk BPMs to uncharted levels.

As well, the UK Subs were already shaking up the genre's formal language in ways that would prove central to later generations of punk and metal—but especially Discharge. Truly the bridge band between punk's first and second waves, the Subs and their rotating drum stool of sticksmen actually possessed the very musical virtuosity disdained by punk orthodoxy; this tendency would poke its head out in intense flashes of spiky brilliance on songs like "Emotional Blackmail." On "Emotional Blackmail," the Subs play in an almost unnatural lockstep. Most startling is the stop/start on-a-dime syncopation of the percussion: staccato bursts of quickly grabbed crash cymbals the primary dynamic accent for emphasis, merging jarringly with the guitar's disarmingly metronomic riff-based groove. "It was like the guitar there was doing what the timpani does in orchestral performances," noted Ian Astbury, early punk adopter and vocalist for post-punk/hard rock tribalists the Cult (and perhaps the Hendrix of the tambourine, it must be noted). Simultaneously, appealingly "primitive" and "exotic" sounding (and easy to play) floor tom-heavy tribal rhythms were also making themselves heard in bands starting from Adam and the Ants all through the post-punk of Killing Joke and Astbury's earlier band, Southern Death Cult (themselves highly influenced by Crass in this regard). All of those strands would be brought together in Tezz's D-beat.

Punk was not unlike other extreme music styles in that, once the extreme aspect was introduced, it would become the dominant *raison d'être* of the music itself. Harder, faster, louder, more angry, more dissonant—at some point in an extreme genre's life, this becomes the only way forward. This has proven true for diverse musical styles spanning heavy metal, drum and bass, and free jazz, and it was certainly true for punk's second wave.

Just as the Ramones and the Damned reduced the Stooges, New York Dolls, and *Nuggets* to its loudest, fastest denominator, so did Discharge and its "UK82" peers (bands like the Exploited, Partisans, Blitz, Anti-Pasti, Abrasive Wheels, and especially Clay Records' labelmates GBH) approximate their primordial influences. More was more in UK82—longer, more garish spiky hair styles (to the point where it approximated the State of Liberty's headgear, hence "liberty spikes"); more egregiously studded and painted leather jackets; more attitude conveying even more pointed and controversial political opinions; more volume, more noise—and more speed, referring to both tempo and illegal drugs. Musical movements have long been tied to intoxicants spanning cocaine and LSD to ecstasy and heroin; as such, punk's second wave was especially amphetamine fueled—you could hear the sulphate in the rapid tempos.

"In the US hardcore scene, Discharge was accepted because they played so fast," notes Moby, the electronic music artist/producer who spent his teens playing in East Coast hardcore bands like Vatican Commandos (and yes, was Flipper's lead singer for one night). "Speed was everything in early hardcore. The music had to be fast, and Discharge was one of the fastest."

The UK82 moment has its fans and detractors. Some consider the period's bands as a sort of eighties hair metal equivalent to seventies punk, exaggerating the aesthetics until they didn't mean the same thing. But that tendency is also why it's proven to be one of the most influential and enduring of punk's formal evolutions. The intensity of the best bands from the second wave has no equivalent in the digital age—and Discharge was by far the best, and most important, of them.

Discharge started as the firstborn spawn of the UK's original punk movement—the band even taking its name from a lyric in the Sex Pistol's "Bodies" ("I'm not a discharge"). According to Tezz Robert's brutal, fascinating confessional memoir *But After the Gig...*, the name "Discharge" was perhaps even more repellent than "Sex Pistols"—and that was exactly the point.

Formed in 1977 in the English Midlands town of Stoke-on-Trent—the UK's longtime pottery capital, referred to in the name of Discharge's indie recording label, Clay—Discharge began as hopelessly derivative Pistols wannabes. That's clear from the music compiled on Discharge's *Early Demos March – June 1977*. In this collection of Discharge's earliest recordings, Discharge's then-frontman Tezz howled a clearly Johnny Rotten-imitating caterwaul over an equally unremarkable, conventional mid-tempo punk chug.

Early Demos March – June 1977 could've been made by probably any number of bands in the UK at the time. Discharge would come into its own sound, though, on its first official release, the 1980 EP *Realities of War*. On *Realities of War*, Tezz moved from center stage to behind the drum stool—replaced on vocals by the band's former roadie, Kelvin "Cal" Morris.

These proved most auspicious choices. "I switched to drums and did the [furiously fast] D-beat," Tezz noted in an interview with *The Guardian*'s Dave Simpson. "The band changed overnight." "That drum beat changes the way you play," Discharge guitarist (and Tezz's brother) Anthony "Bones" Roberts pointed out in an interview with Loudersound.com. "You can't help but get excited by the sound of it. That'd be the basis of what we'd start with, and it makes everything feel so much more urgent, and I definitely reacted to that."

In the new lineup, powered by fresh, unique rhythms, Cal proved a far more powerful and distinctive vocalist and lyricist than Tezz. Cal's chanted scream-cum-growl was more guttural and uncompromisingly raw than anything that had come before, while his explicitly anarchistic, anti-war, deeply political, and radical lyrics were an urgent call to arms the likes of which had no previous equivalent in punk. Crass explored similar themes of social consciousness and radicalism, of course, and served as Cal's primary influence—but Cal's vocals added an urgency, gravitas, and sheer rock and roll wildness to them that wasn't a feature of Crass's more artsy, experimental sonic deconstructions. Tezz also proved something of a savant visionary on drums. Despite (or perhaps because of) his inexperience on the instrument, he ended up pioneering a kind of everyman maximalist minimalism with his take on the D-beat.

"I had never played drums before," Tezz notes in *The Birth of the D-Beat*. "Nearest I came to it was hearing Cozy Powell's 'Dance with the Devil' on the radio and banging along around with me mum's hairbrush." Indeed, flashy seventies rock drummer virtuoso Cozy Powell—who'd made his name playing with musos like Jeff Beck and Ritchie Blackmore, Ozzy-less Black Sabbath, and proggers Emerson, Lake & Powell—proved an unlikely but undeniable influence on punk's innovators. Steve Jones clearly nicked the intro to Sex Pistols' "Holidays in the Sun" from Powell's 1974 UK top 10 hit "Na Na Na"; Powell's other major solo hit, 1973's "Dance with the Devil," also proved a defining influence on Tezz and his evolution of the D-beat rhythm.

"Dance with the Devil" on the surface is about as un-punk as a song could be—a suite-like instrumental interpolation of Jimi Hendrix's psychedelic classic "Third Stone from the Sun" in the form of an extended seventies cock-rock drum solo.

Further analysis, however, reveals how "Dance with the Devil" might've influenced Roberts toward his D-beat innovation with Discharge. For one, it foregrounds drums not as a backing instrument, or even primary driver of the riff; on "Dance with the Devil," the beat of the drums *is* the riff—it's the main hook. Its tribal rhythmic pocket grows increasingly hypnotic in its repetition, which Powell plays with a relentless intensity that seems almost like a superhuman endurance test.

These are all qualities that Tezz would distill into his D-beat innovation—filtering them through an increasingly radical, speed-addled, personally idiosyncratic conception of punk musical tropes. Not just the spine for early Discharge, Tezz's distinctive drum cadences would go on to provide a sonic backbone for a new generation's take on punk. *Realities of War*'s title track is the first example of what we consider proper D-beat today. Tezz commences the song with a quick tribal pattern intro on the floor toms—then switches to the crash cymbal as a ride for the verses, returning to the floor tom motif to set off the chorus. The 132 beats per minute powering "Realities of War" in fact proves two beats per minute slower than "Anarchy in the UK," but it feels three times as fast. Discharge would go on to surpass 160 beats per minute: this was anarchy for 1982, after all, not 1977— this year's model naturally had to break speed records.

"Suddenly, Discharge sounded like a bulldozer," Clay Records founder and Discharge producer Mike Stone also noted to *The Guardian* about his impressions seeing the band's Cal-fronted, D-beat driven incarnation for the first time. "They made the Pistols sound like Take That." "It had to be a certain different tempo," Tezz explains to Spike Smith in *The Birth of the D-Beat*. "No one was playing those outrageous speeds. Velocity is what we wanted, and that's what I done with it."

In addition to its need for speed, UK82 punk was above all about stylizing the almighty riff—isolating it and exaggerating it as the primary musical element in a song. Punk had always been riff and repetition based, in opposition to the melodic, fluid, sonically gorgeous guitar solo excess of mainstream seventies rock; Discharge, though, would take this tendency to its going-for-baroque extreme. In "Realities of War," the drums are a riff, the guitars are a riff, the shouted vocals and truncated lyrics are a riff. After they all combine together—interlocking to create yet another, even more massive and memorable riff—the song is over in a minute, before a conventional pop single would've made it to the first chorus.

The D-beat proved as ramshackle as it was precise. To play it for maximum impact, the musical unit had to be incredibly tight in its interplay, all while playing so hard and fast that the whole enterprise seemed constantly on the verge of violent collapse. And despite veering into near cacophony, Discharge's songs proved incongruously catchy, their screamed refrains and lickety-split syncopations the unlikeliest of earworms.

This was thrilling and new—"Rites of Spring" mixed with "Carmina Burana." Like Stravinsky's convention-shattering masterpiece, Discharge's riff-as-song stylistic innovation proved so radically exhilarating, audiences at their concerts would frequently riot upon hearing it. (This would soon become a staple of Discharge's live shows.) And like Orff's overstuffed dramatic cantata, every moment in Discharge's songs was not just huge, but the hugest possible. Fills in Tezz's D-beat added creative little blasts of ingenuity and variety, but they served entirely to set up the next big change as epically and startlingly as possible. In the uncompromising "It's No TV Sketch," open crash cymbals detonate on nearly every note in the verse; they're allowed to ring out rebelliously before the percussive emphasis switches to a cymbal-free, floor tom-driven tribal cadence, and in the process dynamically setting off Cal's shouted call-and-response gang-vocal chorus.

Hard/soft, loud/quiet, rinse/repeat... What Discharge shared with classical music most, though, was its ability to make music that actually sounded like the subject the song was about. Just as, say, Debussy could impressionistically convey with musical notes and compositional arrangement the qualities of color, or the passing of seasons, Discharge's music sounded like the nuclear war apocalypse described in its lyrics. As such, Discharge D-beat chestnuts like "A Look at Tomorrow" and "Hear Nothing See Nothing Say Nothing" open with proto-blast beats that evoke the industrially metronomic stutter of an automatic weapon, much as Jimi Hendrix did with the guitar part on "Machine Gun." The buzz saw rhythms of the Ramones had become anti-aircraft artillery in Discharge's arsenal. The D-beat wasn't a call to arms anymore—it was the ordnance itself. The unvarying dynamic intensity became a kind of violent blur mimicking the whizz of a surface-to-air missile, sucking the listener into the wake of its exhaust as it blasted past.

Discharge's new stylization of punk tempos dovetailed, probably unwittingly, with the zeitgeist of contemporary minimalist classical and ambient music from the likes of Philip Glass, Steven Reich, and Brian Eno—all of which was deeply repetitive and stripped of romantic orchestral flourish. A famous aphorism from Brian Eno's "Oblique Strategies" is "Repetition is a form of change," and Discharge proved the supreme example of this. The repetitive nature of Tezz's D-beat, mixed with the superhuman physical exertion necessary to maintain its structure, didn't remove variation per se. Instead, within D-beat's precisionist rigor, any even slight variation, nuance, or mistake takes on even greater impact, becoming startlingly monumental when they appear. Even when these variations aren't perceived consciously, they're felt subliminally—that tension decentering listeners further, forcing them to hang onto every snare crack or bass kick as if for dear life. It's like a rollercoaster: the thrill comes in feeling like it might fly off the rails at terrifying speeds, but knowing ultimately it won't—despite the nagging uncertainty and potential for destruction in every abrupt drop, turn, and fall.

The D-beat also distinguished itself from punk's first wave in its embrace of heavy metal as an undeniable influence. After all, the biggest bands of punk's second generation were the Exploited, Discharge, and GBH: the latter two hailed from England's industrial Midlands area, while the former were from Edinburgh, Scotland, *fer fook's sake!* This was the UK equivalent of what's derogatorily referred to in the United States as flyover country; just as in the middle of America, the Midlands always had a thing for unfashionably heavy, primeval rock music. And as punk spread far outward from the sophisticated cultural snobbery of London and Manchester, it became less beholden to influences which were initially *verboten* in the class of 1976.

In early UK punk circles, heavy metal was uncool. Punk was intended, after all, as the enlightened futurist alternative to the sexist cock-rock, egotistical bombast, and blues-rock conformity epitomized by Led Zeppelin, Bad Company, and other hirsute-chested hard rock bands. "I've realized over the years that what we chose as a musical style—if you can call it that—was the destruction of the blues scale," Tezz writes in *But After the Gig...*

Yet bands like Zeppelin and Black Sabbath themselves had deep roots in the Midlands that were challenging to fully extricate. Meet the new boss, same as the old boss: as a budding music enthusiast, Tezz had first been enamored by the riff-centric evil heaviness of Black Sabbath—as well as the fact that they were essentially a local band made good. Black Sabbath were relatable, yet they were heavier and trippier than anything out there. Hawkwind as well may have hailed from prog realms, but there was an edgy countercultural vibe in their grooves that showed up as a latent mutation in punk rockers. As Discharge would later approximate in punk style, Hawkwind raged against the machine by sort of becoming one: an unrelenting, repetitive, near-industrial pulse, and echoes of dystopian urban violence and decay underlay even Hawkwind's most *Kosmiche* space epics.

Indeed, the real X-factor in the D-beat came from Tezz's unabashed love of the most metal band of all, Motörhead—whose mastermind, Lemmy, had been both a member of Hawkwind and was a "Potter" born and raised in Stoke-on-Trent as well. "We all loved Motörhead, but the punks wouldn't admit it," Tezz confesses in his *Guardian* interview. "If I had to pick my favorite bands at the time, three class bands whose work meant everything to me, it would have been the Pistols, Motörhead, and the Subs." He elaborates further on the ingenuity of his unlikely punk-metal hybrid early in the autobiographical arc captured in *But After the Gig…*:

"Me playing the drums was a big part of us creating our new sound. Because I'd been teaching myself to play, I'd been listening to lots of music, lots of different drummers, and I had lots of different influences. Philthy Animal from Motörhead for one, Pete Davies from the UK Subs (a phenomenal drummer whom I recorded an album with later, when I toured the US with the Subs and he was in the band —but that's getting ahead of myself) for another. I'd listen to them, and then I'd head into the rehearsal rooms and practice, and I'd always take someone with me, so that I was always under pressure to make it work, to get it right."

By the late seventies and early eighties, variations on the D-beat pattern had in fact begun revealing themselves in heavy metal's bleeding edge. "Rapid Fire" by Judas Priest, off their 1980 masterpiece *British Steel*, reveals a version of the distinctive D-beat gallop; likewise, as Discharge were developing their version, younger bands like Diamond Head hailing from what was called the "New Wave of British Heavy Metal" embraced stomping D-beat-style syncopation combined and relentless tempos simultaneously. But most of all, it was speedy Motörhead classics like "Overkill," "Iron Fist," "Ace of Spades," "The Hammer," and "Bite the Bullet" that inspired Discharge and peers like GBH to home in on the rhythm and transform it for their own purposes. (Second to Discharge, GBH helped to popularize the D-beat via its genius drummer Wilf's own take on it, which perhaps had a bit more "Ballroom Blitz" in it than Tezz's version.)

D-beat is like art: you know it when you hear it—even if you don't understand why it works so well. Part of the appeal of the D-beat is that in it, Tezz was attempting the impossible and intuitively finding new creative solutions to achieve it. Philthy from Motörhead, for example, got that distinctive pattern from playing with double kick drums; when Roberts was developing the D-beat, he was attempting to approximate Philthy's double-kick technique with just one kick drum—mostly failing, but in the process, creating something new and equally as exciting and wild. "We didn't have the same musical skills, so we went one hundred miles per hour," GBH frontman, Colin Abrahall, noted in *The Guardian*'s D-beat exegesis.

"I think a lot of D-beat honestly happened through the economy of physical motion while trying to make something sound really good," explains Adam Zuckert (who with Final Conflict covered Discharge's "A Look at Tomorrow" on the

1992 compilation *Discharged–From Home Front to War Front*). "It's hard to even count—you literally have to condition your body to play like that, to make it through an hour set."

The D-beat in its way served as a divining rod, a common denominator, a bullshit detector separating those punk bands that had a real creative spark from those that were just going through the motions. Theoretically, the D-beat was nearly the same in each instance, making how you approached and used it reveal inspired creativity (or lack thereof) in high relief. The Buzzcocks' John Maher makes that clear in *The Birth of the D-Beat* when he demonstrates how even subtle nuances in hi-hat attack can create a more dynamic and fluid pattern. "Little movements of the left foot do change the sound of the hi-hat," Maher explains. "A little bit of open on the first note does give it that little extra something."

I myself played guitar in what was arguably Chicago's first D-beat oriented band, Nadsat Rebel (although it must be said that the late, great Pierre Kezdy—rightly renowned for his bass playing in Naked Raygun and Strike Under—wore the first Discharge T-shirt in the city, bought for him by his brother, Effigies lead singer John Kezdy, on a trip to England). I was a true-believer evangelist for Discharge—I actually had the Discharge trio of skulls logo painted on the back of my leather jacket, under which I would typically sport a Motörhead shirt in imitation of my idols. True story: I actually played Discharge for Dave Grohl in 1982 at his cousin Tracey's house. It was the first time Dave had ever heard music like that, and you could see his eyes light up with discovery as the D-beat kicked in. This was a new world of music Discharge had opened up with this radical sound, and Grohl was immediately a convert. Around the country, starting in the early eighties, regional punk bands like Final Conflict, Crucifix, Neurosis, and Battalion of Saints began similarly reveling in

Discharge's D-beat, using it to find their own style. Meanwhile, when Discharge attempted to go full metal and leave the D-beat behind, it controversially didn't take as well. The original D-beat Discharge was simply heavier and more radical than anything else. You didn't listen to Discharge because they were metal, or even punk—you did so because what they offered sonically was so unique, it just couldn't be found anywhere else.

"The originality, just the sheer energy of it all, the musicality, the cool risk taking—nobody else could bring all of those things together with the intensity, speed, and power Discharge did," Zuckert says. "From the drums and the visual imagery, to the singing and radical messages in the lyrics, the sheer devotion to the style was fucking awesome. Discharge did something so unique and magical and cool—so raw and stripped down, and ahead of its time—that it still doesn't sound dated. It's timeless."

And global. Finland, Japan, Eastern Europe, New Jersey... Bands continue to form all around the world following Discharge's template, united by the brotherhood of D-beat. Against all odds, the D-beat endures and continues to inspire. "We constructed this thing called the D-beat, which goes on to conquer Norway and Sweden and gets used by a load of hardcore punk bands," Tezz reflects early in *But After the Gig...* "But I did it first. It gave us something special, something which made people stop and take notice. I can't listen to those bands and say, 'That's what we invented.' But I know we changed the direction of music."

In terms of punk drumming hallmarks, **Matt Diehl** *played Dave Grohl the first punk rock he'd ever heard. Otherwise, Diehl is known for his books spanning hip-hop crime to one-hit wonders and pop culture writing for* Rolling Stone, The New York Times, *and the like.*

1984: ROCK AGAINST REAGAN
(*DREADNAUGHT* CHAPTER EXCERPT)

By D. H. Peligro

B ACK IN SAN FRANCISCO, Dead Kennedys rehearsed about three or four days a week for about three hours at a time, developing new material and then going on tour or playing small gigs. Musically, we worked out arrangements in rehearsals. In other bands, the drummers typically twiddle their thumbs while waiting for the guitarist and the bass player to work it out. Not me. I was involved and throwing out suggestions left and right. Most drum parts came naturally to me and, since I could play guitar and sing, I did my part and then some. If I had a song that I thought would fit in, I would bring it in with all of its parts: guitar parts, bass parts, lyrics, melodies, and of course drums. It was very nerve-racking since (Jello) Biafra was so brilliant with lyrics, but then again so was I. He'd hum stuff and we'd have to figure out how to make it music, then transpose it up and down to fit the range of Biafra's voice. Biafra would come in with ideas, but he would have to process them through us. His timing was pretty off, from my point of view, and by the way he explained things, it seemed as though they wouldn't work. First, I'd try to understand what the hell he was talking about, and then I'd have to fit it into a workable time signature. Then we would start the transposing process again.

This was an intense period politically, and Biafra created quite a controversy. Reagan, a very shaky president, entered the War on Drugs while the government was giving money to the Contras in South America, which in turn helped flood the USA with cheaper cocaine, creating the crack epidemic. This fueled the fire for Blood and Crip gang wars in the inner city. Reagan also closed many mental institutions, which filled the streets of San Francisco with untreated mental patients. Everywhere we played there was a huge police presence. I was sure the CIA kept tabs on us. I was getting stopped and searched and pulled over way too much for it to be any kind of a coincidence. I think the cops set me up on a weed bust in Hunters Point while I was doing a favor for a friend, Wild Bill, an ex-Vietnam vet. Because of that I got a felony rap, which I still pay for today. My record's been expunged so I can vote and serve jury duty, but I can't legally own a gun.

<>

DEAD KENNEDYS PLAYED ROCK Against Reagan, a huge free outdoor show. There were police on all the roofs, completely surrounding us. I didn't know what the fuss was about but there were a lot of people there. There was so much security that Biafra started shouting, "Look above you, see them all on the roof? That's the police state!" It was moments like this I saw what I was really involved with. It wasn't all drugs and parties, leather jackets with studs and bristles, mohawks, safety pins, BO, and peg pants—it was Martial Law seeping in, and I would hammer the message via drumming, as if I were sending some secret African tribal message to everyone tuned into the vibe. I felt like I was high on fire. I would break my sticks during every song, so I kept extra sticks in the lug nut on the kick drum. Some kids thought it was cute to jump onstage, skank around, and try to steal my spare sticks. I was playing fast, but it was nothing for me to reach out, grab the sticks out of their hands, and not miss a beat.

After *Plastic Surgery Disasters*, the punk rock scene in San Francisco started to heat up. It revolved around a few venues: Mabuhay Gardens, On Broadway, Valencia Tool & Die, the Farm, 10th St. Hall, Ruthie's in Oakland/Berkley Square, the Elite Club (now the Fillmore), the Stone, Keystone, and the Vats. Temple Beautiful (which was later named the Temple) was closed by then—incidentally, this is where Jim Jones brainwashed people, and where they gathered before going to Guyana and drinking poisoned Kool-Aid. Punk bands recorded wherever they could to stretch a dollar. Of course, we recorded *In God We Trust, Inc.* at Target Video, *Plastic Surgery Disasters* with Tom Wilson at Mobius Music, *Frankenchrist* and *Bedtime for Democracy* were filmed at Hyde Street Studios in San Francisco. In Studio D, we recorded *Frankenchrist* with John Cuniberti. We also recorded *Bedtime for Democracy* with him in Studio C, and I think Garry Creiman helped out at some point. Garry also did the late night sessions with the Sluglords that I recorded with Bruno de Smartass (a.k.a. Steve DeMartis). The tracks I played on were "Yakety Trumpet" and "Free Food." I also did guest vocals on "Work for It"; if you listen closely, my voice is the first one you hear saying, "Uh…we're being taken for a ride."

Back in the early eighties, the Vats was part of the old Hamm's Brewery off of South Van Ness and Sixteenth. It had been abandoned for a while and became a squat for punk rockers and general misfits. Someone jack hammered through the concrete wall and somehow got the electricity running. Bands came in and put carpet down in a few of the rooms to make rehearsal studios.

Everybody used to go there, and I would hang out with all kinds of bands coming and going. It was an insane place. You would walk in total darkness, squishing through puddles of old beer left over from the brewery. I can still smell that smell today when I walk by an old dumpster. There were entire floors you couldn't go to—empty, scary, little cave-like rooms and then these huge vats twenty feet deep into the floor.

This is when I started getting to know Mark Byron. He was a real mechanical whiz at the time and had access to generators, which we needed at the Vats. So, Mark brought in this 5,000 watt generator, and bands started playing outdoor daytime Sunday shows. Mark would pull up on his Harley with a skateboard bungee corded to his sissy bar and work the generator. Everybody got along for the most part. Mostly people were drunk or tweaking, but the cops left us alone, and for the most part the bands would play all day.

San Francisco is so small we just fit together in a dysfunctional kind of way. The crew from Texas and MDC were good friends with us for a long time. Al from MDC actually made the first DK logo that I had on my kick drum.

Later we became friends with the Dicks. Their lead singer Gary Floyd was a trippy queen. They played the Vats along with bands like Dirty Rotten Imbeciles (DRI), and we did the Rock Against Reagan tour in Texas with MDC and the Dicks in the relentless, sweltering heat and humidity of the Southern summer. After touring the South, we befriended east coast bands like Mission of Burma from Boston, Kraut from NYC, Bad Brains, False Prophets, Minor Threat, and Government Issue from DC, and our Canadian friends D.O.A., Pointed Sticks, and S.N.F.U. There were So Cal troublemakers like TSOL, the Vandals, and Circle Jerks who we also played with from time to time.

The homegrown San Francisco bands were the Sluglords, Frightwig, Hellations, and Flipper—one of the rattiest sloth-dirge punk bands ever. Flipper's drummer, Steve de Pace, was also in the legendary punk band Negative Trend with our friend Will Shatter. Steve and I later became roommates at Mission-A, as well as serious friends and partners in crime. Steve would go on to play with me in the Jungle Studs.

Also, there was Bad Posture with Eddie and Emilio, some of the first Mexican punk rockers from Brownsville, Texas. They were always broke, bumming beer and weed, and we had to buy them strings, but they were great players, and they came as a pair. Bruno had a joke back then. They'd walk into the studio and we'd say, "What are Eddie and Emilio in a box?" Everyone knew. "A pair of brown loafers!"

Jeff 4Way was the singer for Bad Posture and wore about a seven-foot-tall Mohawk. No, my bad, he was about seven foot tall and wore a Mohawk. He got his name 4Way working security for Bow Wow Wow at the Kabuki Theater when someone gave him a four-way hit of acid. The thing is, it's a four-way hit. You're only supposed to take one, but no, he took the whole thing and lost his mind for a few days, hence the name 4Way. Bad Posture's hits included "Goddamn Motherfuckin' Son of a Bitch," "Signal 30" (which was also done by Sluglords), and my all-time favorite "Time for Smack!" John Sidel was their drummer, and Emilio was the bass player; Eddie and Bruno played guitar.

Woody played bass in Sluglords, and most of them lived on and off at the House of Morons on South Van Ness between Fifteenth and Sixteenth Streets. I spent most of my time there, and Woody would later be in the Jungle Studs with me. Tony and Fred Dickerson, Steve DePace, and Bruno de Smartass were all in the Jungle Studs at one time or another.

I started my own band called the Hellations. I was the songwriter, vocalist, and guitar player. I had this girl, Megan, on bass, and this crazy girl named Jane on drums. Jane didn't do any drugs; she was just genuinely crazy and a real artist. She painted a gigantic mural on the outside of the house with various collages of the Beatles. Her room was filled with dolls and stacks and stacks of comic books. She would make these brilliant flyers, combining collages out of comic books and her own artwork.

Later on, Tony C. and I organized the Jungle Studs with Steve DePace on drums. We were just biting off of everything in our music. We tried to be a cross between the Time, Prince, and Van Halen but ended up sounding like Flipper meets Peter Gabriel. It was weird but it was fun and kind of funky. Fred Dickerson was with us for a while. He brought in a seventies rock influence; I had the punk aggressive vibe, Steve DePace had this laid back, depressed Flipper beat. I tried to push up the energy, get Steve up to speed, but he just didn't play like that. I knew it was just a fun project. I doubted that it would ever be put out, but Alternative Tentacles actually did release the album in 1986.

D. H. Peligro *is the longtime and current drummer for legendary San Francisco punk band Dead Kennedys. In 1988, he joined the Red Hot Chili Peppers, replacing Jack Irons, before being fired for drug and alcohol issues. He has released three albums with his band Peligro:* Peligro *(released in 1995 on Jello Biafra's Alternative Tentacles record label);* Welcome to America; *and* Sum of Our Surroundings, *which won Rock Album of the Year at the 2004 American Independent Music Awards. He also recently recorded a cover of Jimi Hendrix's "Purple Haze," which was nominated for a Grammy Award. He lives in Los Angeles.*

MIKE WATT ON GEORGE HURLEY

Interviewed by S. W. Lauden

AS THE BASSIST/SONGWRITER FOR both the Minutemen and fIREHOSE, Mike Watt has continually redefined the boundary-pushing possibilities of punk rock. His consistent rhythmic coconspirator in both those bands was George Hurley, one of the most original drummers to emerge from the late-seventies LA scene. Whether jamming with D. Boon or ed fROMOHIO (a.k.a. Edward Crawford), Watt and Hurley brought a wide range of influences and unique perspectives to the incredible music they created in both powerhouse trios. Below are some highlights from my conversation with Mike Watt about playing with his longtime drummer and friend, George Hurley.

How did you first meet George Hurley?

Me, D. Boon, and George are class of seventy-six, San Pedro High. Georgie was a happening dude on campus…he built his own surfboards, but he wanted to learn drums. So, he got a drum set right after high school, right when the [punk] movement started. He went to live on the beach in Hawaii and almost got killed surfing those big ass waves so he said, "Fuck this, I'm getting out of surfboards." He turned the shed where he used to build them into a prac[tice] pad. So, he bought the Who's *My Generation* and Billy Cobham's *Spectrum*. And he got some headphones and taught himself to play drums from those two fucking records.

The movement wasn't just some style of music for us; it was about trying to make your own songs. We didn't know anybody in the seventies who wrote their own songs; everybody was just trying to copy off of records. That's why we were attracted to the movement.

You played in a band with D. Boon and George Hurley before the Minutemen, right?

We did this band in 1978 called the Reactionaries. That's where I wrote my first songs, and they were pretty shitty. You have to start somewhere, you don't just jump on a skateboard and start pulling ollies—well, some dudes do, but not Watt. I was stumbling and learning by doing. Finally, D. Boon left that band in the fall of seventy-nine.

The beginning of 1980 was when D. Boon wanted to make the real band [the Minutemen], but actually we didn't have Georgie on drums at first. We had this welder guy that D. Boon met at Harbor College named Frank Tonche. He only lasted two gigs. He lived in a little house in his sister's backyard, so he had a prac pad, which was essential. He came from a Polish polka band. He was a nice guy and could play good, but the scene freaked him out so he bailed after the second gig. But Greg Ginn [Black Flag/SST Records] was at that gig, and he wanted us to be SST 002.

Georgie had joined this band up in Hollywood called Hey Taxi! in the meantime, but they had broken up. So Georgie was available. He learned the songs in three fucking weeks and that became SST 002, *Paranoid Time*.

Then Black Flag taught us how to tour... What we found out was having a guy like George Hurley on tour was incredibly essential. Intelligence isn't just learning facts, it's being able to put your brain in a *sitch*—and Georgie was the guy you wanted with you in a situation where almost anything could fucking happen.

How did the Minutemen come up with their unique sound?

D. Boon thought the Minutemen was political…. [He] thought the lyrics were just thinking out loud. The political part was bringing the drums and the bass up equal with the guitar. Making it egalitarian. It wasn't a rhythm section, it was about all three of us making an interesting conversation.

I learned a lot of it from Doug Clifford's drumming in Creedence [Clearwater Revival]. When I met D. Boon, the only fucking rock band he knew was Creedence. He didn't know about Cream, or any of that shit. But Doug Clifford was a smart-ass drummer; he's gonna tell you when the verse comes, or the bridge and the chorus—all the nuance. Georgie totally got into all of that. If nobody tells you that your instrument has limitations, you let the freak flag fly. And that's what Georgie did.

How did George Hurley's style inform your playing?

I composed a lot on the bass, so the bass part's coming first. I have to adjust when I bring it to Georgie because, well, he just made it groovy. It's like James Jamerson with Benny Benjamin. Or Bootsy [Collins] with Clyde Stubblefield. Just you being responsible to the feel…it's only clay that you throw on that wheel. Georgie spins that fucking wheel. And he was also a big picture guy, like Doug Clifford. He learned the tunes. Minutemen tunes were short, but he learned them inside and out.

A lot of this shit we learned from R&B, like D. Boon getting all trebly and playing all clipped to give the drums and bass more room. That's from R&B players, you know? Listen to Curtis Mayfield records. That's where we got this stuff. I mean, you could hear a lot of bass on the rock and roll coming out of England—for example, Cream and Jack Bruce, a big influence on me. Geezer Butler. Trevor Bolder. Pete Quaife from the Kinks. And Chas Chandler from the Animals. Those producers got it, but over here it was all muddy and shit.

Listen to Trevor Bolder and Woody Woodmansey. Listen to Geezer Butler and Bill Ward—especially *Paranoid, Master of Reality, Volume 4.* Oh my god. Jack Bruce with Ginger Baker, right? So, if you ask me how I'm influenced by George Hurley, listen to those guys. All that kind of stuff is where I learned from, and Georgie was into it, too.

Georgie could probably be like a Hal Blaine, right? A thirty thousand song session man, because he's got that kind of musical acumen, but I think where the Minutemen was the strongest was the three-way tie.

Can you tell me the difference between the songwriting for fIREHOSE and the Minutemen?

Well, I didn't have D. Boon. Big difference. See, here's the funky thing about fIREHOSE—I don't know how to do bands really, so I tried doing Minutemen again. Edward [Crawford] finds my number in a phone book—I didn't know you had to pay to be unlisted…. That first day he came to my pad we tried writing songs, and we did. Like "Brave Captain" and "The Candle and the Flame," shit that showed up on the first record.

I also had to use a lot of Dos songs. The first side band I ever tried to do was Dos. It was near the end of the Minutemen; I didn't know that was going to be the end. So, me and K [Kira Roessler] start this band of just two basses. I put all my music through D. Boon, but I thought I'd try this one weird thing. So, when Edward comes, I don't know him. I don't know how to write songs for him, so I throw him songs I wrote for K and Dos.

Then, like the old days with D. Boon, we let Georgie come in. And Georgie comes up with his parts like he did. You work with him at the prac, right? "Okay, Georgie. Here's where we go to the chorus. Here's where go to the bridge." That's how he developed his parts. You didn't really have to tell him, he experimented. It was Petri dish time. This was a learn-by-doing band.

George Hurley is definitely one of the most unique drummers I've ever seen play live.

Georgie Hurley is one of these guys, like Nicola Tesla. He's an innovator. That's why people make fun of drummers, because they're afraid of the power.... But Georgie had another visual thing that I should talk about. He had this trippy haircut we called "the unit." He'd start swinging this thing around and it was like a helicopter blade. It was like a ponytail but coming out of the front of his head. So, that was pretty unique.

When he was composing, he liked to start with the hi-hat and then work his way down, but he was way into these things called bells. You know the bell part of the cymbal? So, he had a little forest, like three or four of these little fuckers. Also, he had some Remo Rototoms—he had some of those on the starboard side, and on the port side he had a little forest of different sized bells. Then he had a little ten-inch splash [cymbal] in between.

Because of the jazz thing, Georgie was really interested in polyrhythm. But he was not into the genre thing, he liked mixing things up.

A lot of great punk drummers came out of LA. Who are some favorites?

I got to say, there were some other great drummers here in our scene. Don Bolles from the Germs is a pretty incredible drummer.

Steve Perkins from Porno for Pyros and Jane's Addiction was a little later, but a really great drummer. Billy Stevenson from the Descendents, who's also a good songwriter. Robo [Black Flag] had a very key signature style, like those rolls he did in "Police Story." ...And for a while Chuck Biscuits [D.O.A.] was in Black Flag. He's really good.

There were some kicking drummers, and this was very important to Georgie. He liked that. He would always talk drums with the other band... Derrick Bostrom [Meat Puppets]. Grant Hart [Hüsker Dü]. Brother drummers. There's stuff to learn from each other.

When you think about George Hurley's drumming, are there certain songs that stand out?

Like, for example, "Search"—that drum intro. How key! That's signature shit. You know? You have to pay people to come up with stuff like that. [Laughs.] Georgie was just matter of fact. He's reacting to me and D. Boon. "Here, play it for me... Play it again...Okay. I got it." That's why a lot of our composition time was spent with Georgie, not with each other.

I tell you, that part in "The Anchor," where he also writes the words. Georgie learned to find where my bass motifs were so he didn't always have to put the kick on the one. Also a big fan of reggae, right? So you make room for the other parts.

He's got the weirdest kick drum pattern in "Brave Captain." That offbeat shit... It's so bizarre, right? But it works! It pushes that song. In fact, that song got used for skate videos. I had kids tell me they learned to skate to that song. And Georgie did that. It's so unique. Right? Because it's gotta be grooving if you want to be on the skateboard and be moving. If you isolate the kick drum on that song it sounds so insane, but in the big picture it's aiding and abetting like a motherfuck. Which is what you want to do, right? I'm trying to do the same thing with the bass—aid and abet on the tune.

And he could play slow, like "History Lesson Part II." With the sidestick and shit. He's doing dialog, he's in conversation. It's not just sleepwalk, cruise control, Xerox machine shit. He's actually in the ring with you. In the booth!

If you met a young musician starting their first punk band, what advice would you give them about finding a drummer?

Maybe let them choose you. That's what Georgie did. Everybody was like, "Why's this guy playing with them?"

The other thing is, get rid of that hierarchy shit. Drummer means coconspirator. Get that through your head. That old hierarchy is lame. One thing the movement did—and it helped out bass players, too—you're not the stupidest guy in the band, you're not a guy who hangs out with musicians. You *are* a musician. Once you get that kind of respect, you might end up with some good candidates for your band.

The drummer is not the expendable guy, he's the fucking heart in the center of the rock and roll universe.

YOU'RE PRETTY GOOD FOR A GIRL

By Lynn Perko-Truell

I GREW UP IN Miami, Florida, where I was a classically trained pianist, who did public and private recitals into my middle school years. At age twelve, I moved to Reno, Nevada. Once into my teens, I quit the piano lessons and found more joy listening to rock music. My most memorable listening experiences happened with Led Zeppelin, along with the Rolling Stones, the Who, the Police, David Bowie, Neil Young, and Cream. Even though I had no idea I would soon become a drummer, my favorite musicians were John Bonham, Charlie Watts, Stewart Copeland, and Ginger Baker.

My friend, Helen Pardy-Johnson, worked in a record store. One day I went in to browse, and she told me she was going to sing for a band. They needed a drummer and she suggested that I do it; I agreed. Shortly after I went to my first punk rock show and saw 7 Seconds, the Wrecks had their first practice in the family room of Bessie Oakley's house. She played bass and Jone Stebbins played guitar. Since I didn't have any drums, we pulled in a couple of big plastic garbage cans from Bessie's garage, turned them upside down, and used them. The raw and rudimentary sounds of guitars, Helen yelling/singing, and me banging plastic sounded pretty cool. I realized playing punk music meant expressing yourself however you wanted to; playing even if you didn't know how. I just played beats that I could pull off or that I could play fast enough. It was amazing that it was so easy to suddenly be in a band and have a "sound." After a couple of months, I got a real drum set, a Ludwig Club Kit in oyster black and blue—our decided band colors, because we got bruised from thrashing.

We were our own inspiration in the beginning. We were bonded by our lyrics and the fact that we were all girls in a band, which was relatively unprecedented in our own experience of rock bands. The geographical isolation and small size of Reno allowed for an insular and inclusive scene for me to blossom in. It allowed for self-discovery and felt nonjudgmental compared to what we heard about in bigger city scenes. We wrote songs that expressed our disinterest in mainstream society. Our snarl of vocals and instruments gave us power. Proving ourselves as girls that could rock was not our primary purpose—we just *were* girls intrigued by the possibilities of punk rock's music and ideas. Even before my first punk rock show, I knew I wasn't ready for college. I wanted something different and punk became my direction. It was powerful and gave me a purpose and path at sixteen. I had a new identity as Lynn Lust (we all had punk rock names). I began writing songs and lyrics, doing photo shoots, and practicing a couple times a week.

The Wrecks' first show was in October of 1980 at Reno's Rad House—a soundproofed garage equipped with a stage and PA in the back of a rented house that was also a party and crash pad. Because Reno was between the Bay Area and Salt Lake City, many touring American and Canadian punk and hardcore bands passed through, and I watched a lot of their drummers trying to figure out how I should play the drums. On a Wrecks sneak-away trip (from our parents) to see Redd Kross at San Francisco's

On Broadway, I saw my first true inspiration in their drummer Janet Housden. She was the first girl I had ever seen play drums live, and I fought my way through the crowd to the front of the stage to intensely study her playing.

Over the eighteen months we were together, we played with D.O.A., Black Flag, T.S.O.L., 7 Seconds, and more. In 1982, we recorded, packaged, and sent out our own nine-song cassette demo called *Teenage Jive*—the artwork black and blue. Our song "Punk is an Attitude" is on the double album *Not So Quiet on the Eastern Front*, a punk rock and hardcore album put together by the subculture zine *Maximumrocknroll* and released by Alternative Tentacles.

Our last show was July 3, 1982, at the West End Community Center in Vancouver, BC, opening for Black Flag and Saccharine Trust. All the bands were using Black Flag's amps and drums. We were nervous with the big crowd and expectations to see this all-girl band. Black Flag's roadie, Mugger, offered to tune our guitars before stage time, but instead detuned them as a practical joke. Our first song sounded awful. Luckily most Wrecks songs were only one to two minutes long, so we got back in tune as quick as we could—but we were thrown off and already being verbally challenged by the audience. The show was a bit of a calamity. Mugger intentionally tried to make fools of us...I'm guessing he wouldn't have done that to a band of teenage boys.

<>

I MOVED TO SAN Francisco at the end of 1982, and in 1983 I met Gary Floyd through a mutual friend. His band, the Dicks, formed in Texas but he wanted to reform it in San Francisco. He asked me to try out. I heard there were three other guys trying out too, so I knew I had to come in strong, confident, and prepared. At some point, the challenge to be better than guys at playing drums crept in and greatly inspired me.

At the time I was practicing at the Vats, an infamous punk live/work/practice place in San Francisco that was once a brewery. There was a guy there, likely a speed freak, but he was also a drummer. He knew I was going to try out for the Dicks and asked if he could watch me practice some songs. This fellow ended up having a huge impact on my playing style. After watching a couple of songs, he said, "Don't care about how you look or if your mascara is running." (Or maybe he told me my mascara was running—I can't exactly remember, but there was something about mascara.) "Sit in the music and play. Just do whatever you gotta do to get through it." Those were powerful words from a stranger, and I credit him for my abandon while playing drums.

In 1984, I went on my first American tour with the (SF) Dicks. We toured the Midwest and east coast with D.O.A. We played a few actual nightclubs, like the Metro in Chicago—and the legendary punk clubs the Satyricon in Portland, Oregon, and City Gardens in Trenton, New Jersey—but mostly we played a lot of garage-type places with low-hanging ceilings (Gary called them "fire traps"), spending nights on living room floors of promoters and fans across the country. We traveled in a van with the Tile Man logo on it because we bought it cheap from a floor-tile installer. I drove in the smaller towns and over the US/Canadian borders because we *always* got pulled over. Being an eclectic bunch of misfits, we felt a female driver would create less problems with police and locals.

On tour, I realized how bouncers and other band roadies increased my determination to prove myself. I was often regarded as a groupie and many times had to talk my way backstage or send the doorman off to find another band member to let me backstage. Stagehands and roadies sometimes ignored me or snickered at me, so most nights I could hardly wait for sound check or stage time to get my revenge upon them by dominating the drum set. All their doubting gazes gave me determination, strength, and power, mentally and physically. After a while, I heard more and more "you're pretty good for a girl." A few years ago, I got a DM on social media from a man who told me that he was in the opening band for us in a basement in Brooklyn, New York, and he had said to me at the time, "You are the most exciting female drummer I've ever seen," to which I responded, "I just want to be the best drummer you've ever seen." He said my response never left him and "had an effect on the way (he) raised his daughters."

The members of the Dicks were not close, but I bonded deeply with Gary Floyd. He encouraged me to try out for the Dicks, chose me, and defended me out on the road from the occasionally aggressive and verbally abusive punk boys, and yeah, even a few girls. At a headlining show at the Berkeley Square, I was jumped in a bathroom by the DMR girls—a feminist punk gang in Berkeley—who thought I didn't look punk enough to be at a Dicks show. I made it out of the bathroom, but not before they pushed me around and ripped the shirt off my back as I ran out the door.

The Dicks released a three-song single on R Radical Records, run by Dave Dictor of MDC. We had the infamous Spot from SST Records at the board as the final mixer/producer, recording live performances with no overdubs. It was a party event when a band went to record back then. Many MDC and Dicks friends were hanging at the studio and are included in the ending chorus of "No Fuckin' War," a serious and somber song that was one of the more popular anthems of the time. It was included as the soundtrack to a *Thrasher Magazine* skate video.

In 1984, the Dicks played a Rock Against Reagan show in the parking lot of what was then the Moscone Convention Center in San Francisco where the Democratic National Convention was being held. During "No Fuckin' War" the stage became overcrowded with people grabbing mics to sing the chorus, roaming, and stagediving. It was an exciting time, but the memory of a strong skinhead presence still makes me cringe. We as a band were peaceful people, using art to express our views, but our hardcore sound attracted an aggressive crowd.

In 1985, we recorded the album *These People* with Klaus Flouride from the Dead Kennedys as producer. We did some touring but mostly stuck to shows in SF and LA, including two at the Olympic Auditorium. The first Olympic show was with MDC, Social Distortion, and the headliners, Discharge. Gary was concerned about the rumored intense audience, so he gave himself a mohawk the day we left for LA hoping to fit in and lessen the degree of spit and verbal abuse. Inexplicably, we ran out of gas on the way down to LA and missed our spot in the lineup. The promoter said we could play *after* Discharge, which we did, probably suffering even more animosity from the crowd because of it. In watching videos of that show, I note two things: how fast I could play, and the number of punks from the audience pacing and jumping from the stage. The second time at the Olympic was with Fishbone and Dead Kennedys, which, unbeknownst to us, would be our last show. Due to the aggressive and sometimes violent factions of the scene—skinheads, Nazi-punks, and drunks—our fun and passion was replaced with fear and discomfort. There was no point for the Dicks to carry on.

That was the end of me playing hardcore punk. Gary and I immediately began talking about starting a band where we didn't need to be bound to the rules of any music genre. In 1986, we found a kindred spirit in Ben Cohen and began writing songs for our newly formed band, Sister Double Happiness. Mikey Donaldson, from the Offenders, rounded out our sound, which I describe as heavy blues-rock with a splash of grunge. I flourished as a drummer with SDH because I now had the space for fills, dramatic pauses, and a heavy emotional attack. We released records on SST, Sub Pop USA (Singles Club), and Europe, Reprise, and Innerstate Records. We toured Europe and the US multiple times, both as headliner and as the opener for Nirvana, Soundgarden, the Replacements, Dinosaur Jr., 4 Non-Blondes, and others. During this time, I worked on a movie project with Paul Westerberg, and via J Mascis, played UK's TV show *The Word* with Dinosaur Jr. (their drummer was injured). With no official break-up, SDH stopped performing in 1996.

I met Roddy Bottum in 1984 when the Dicks played a Squatters' Rights concert at City Hall in San Francisco. Roddy was playing keyboards with the band Trial. Over the years we became close friends, and in 1995, we started chatting about starting a new band. He and I were interested in pushing our musical abilities by trying new instruments and writing and singing pop songs. He knew Will Schwartz from LA and Jone (Wrecks) was now my roommate after her move to SF. We made a demo-tape in 1995 and signed to Slash Records and released our first record as Imperial Teen in 1996. We've released six records, and over many years toured the states numerous times—as a headliner or opening for the White Stripes, the Breeders, Lush, the Lemonheads, Hole, Pink, and others. We also played a few European festivals including Isle of Wight Festival, and have had several music placements in movie soundtracks, TV shows, and TV ads. Although I play several instruments in Imperial Teen, my main one is still the drums. With our more poppy sound, my drumming approach and style did change—becoming crisper and more succinct yet retaining space for powerful tom fills and crescendos.

Punk rock and hardcore helped me discover a fierce passion, a part of me that I may never have known. The experiences I had in my early years behind the kit helped create my identity, drum style, and a true expression of self and power that I could carry into any genre of music, ultimately giving me courage, confidence, and contentment. The bond of both music as a movement and the family of musicians and friends I met along the way remain constant and precious.

Lynn Perko-Truell *is a founding member of and currently plays with Imperial Teen. She was a founding member and drummer of Sister Double Happiness, drummer for the SF Dicks, and all-girl hardcore band The Wrecks.*

HOW I GOT THE BEAT

By Laura Bethita Neptuna

IT'S NOT ALWAYS OBVIOUS who has had the greatest influence on a musician. I'm a drummer in an all-girl surf band called the Neptunas with some not-so-obvious drumming heroes. Bill Stevenson of the Descendents and Black Flag, Keith Moon of the Who, and Clem Burke of Blondie are a few of my major influences. But the drummer who stands out most for me is Gina Schock of the Go-Go's. We come from different worlds and our playing styles are different, but her impact on my path as a drummer is massive.

The Go-Go's first record, *Beauty and The Beat,* came out in spring of 1981. I was fifteen years old and it became a Go-Go's year for me. I wore the grooves out on my copy of that record and saw the Go-Go's live at the Greek Theater in October and at my high school in Palos Verdes, California, in December. It was at those live shows that I came to understand girls could, and did, play rock music. My soul was imprinted with the dream of doing what Gina did. The obsession with playing music was lodged in my spirit, though it would take a decade before it manifested itself. There are so many things about the Go-Go's and Gina that are at the core of how and why I've played drums in two all-girl bands, Ballgagger and the Neptunas.

I'VE ALWAYS THOUGHT OF Gina Schock as a warrior. Her brother took her to her first rock show—the Who and Led Zeppelin—when she was eleven. It was then and there she knew exactly what she was going to do with her life. She wasn't sure what instrument she'd play but she knew she would play rock and roll. Gina became part of the Fells Point scene in Baltimore, joining her first band at thirteen. Her first drum kit was a Japanese Lido Supreme. She was in Baltimore's first punk rock/new wave band, Scratch-n-Sniff. She hung out at John Waters' protégé Edith Massey's thrift store on Broadway, playing drums for Edie & the Eggs. When Gina was twenty-one, after Edie & the Eggs shows in New York, Los Angeles, and San Francisco, Gina packed everything she owned into her father's pick-up truck and left for Los Angeles because it was what felt right to her.

I was always inspired by Gina's drive. She saw the Go-Go's play at a party and thought they were great. Shortly thereafter, she became their drummer. When Gina first joined, they only practiced once every couple of weeks. Gina brought focus, drive, discipline, and determination to the Go-Go's and demanded they practice four or five nights a week. The band quickly got better through all their practicing together and their music evolved into the great pop songs I came to love.

I've always thought Gina's drum hooks were a key part of Go-Go's songs. She doesn't read drum music, instead writing her parts based on what she feels the song is asking for. Every note in each song is figured out during the songwriting process with her bandmates. I love that she doesn't like to mess with what works and never improvises when playing live. Gina eventually upgraded her kit, recording all the Go-Go's records on (and touring with) a Rodger's kit with the same WFL 1957 snare she found in a Boston pawn shop. She also developed a habit of feeling the sticks before playing live, using a heavier stick for her left hand.

As a lifelong fan, these are details I find compelling about her playing. She is such a physical drummer, with every part of her body playing the song (I noticed this about Keith Moon and Clem Burke, too). Her mouth is usually moving, and it looks like she's counting the beats, but she's not. She's just in it, deep.

<>

THE FIRST ROCK AND roll show I attended was AC/DC's *Back In Black* tour. After that, I became fascinated with rock and pop music. I quickly developed my everlasting attraction to melody and hooks in music, which led me to the love of surf and other upbeat music like the Ventures and the Go-Go's. I looked everywhere for biographical information about rock musicians— especially the female ones—reading press and listening to the radio. The Go-Go's were an LA band, and since I grew up there, I heard about them early and often. Their popularity provided me with lots of access to information about them and about Gina.

As a teenager, I listened feverishly to Rodney Bingenheimer's Sunday night radio show on KROQ. The Go-Go's were one of the bands Rodney talked about, which thrilled and inspired me. I began dreaming of playing drums in my own band after I saw the Go-Go's twice in 1981. Knowing they wrote and played their own songs was a huge influence on me, and I loved that the drummer was a girl! I thought maybe I could do it, too.

It wasn't until the nineties that my sister, Julie, and I created our first band, Ballgagger. I started with a Tama Rock Star kit (a Japanese kit, like Gina started with) and played with my sticks inverted using the butt ends, leveraging the weight of the sticks to hit harder (similar to Gina's favoring a heavier stick for her snare hand). Using Gina as my role model, I played with all my might, using my entire body. My drum parts were completely invented out of feel and what the song needed.

Our band, Ballgagger, was the first all-girl band to hail from LA's legendary South Bay punk rock scene. It was the same scene where I'd gotten to see countless Descendents, Black Flag, Minutemen, the Last, and Redd Kross shows while growing up. I was focused and determined, pushing my band to bring music to people's lives like other bands had done for me, bands like the Go-Go's. We played a lot of shows, put out a record on Theologian Records—the same Hermosa Beach record label that launched Pennywise—and we toured all over the United States.

That experience later led me to joining one of my favorite surf bands, an all-girl trio called the Neptunas. I have played in the Neptunas ever since, recording many records and performing across the US, Europe, and Mexico. Playing drums has given me the most amazing experiences of my life, in many ways thanks to seeing Gina Schock play with the Go-Go's when I was a teenager.

◆▸

GINA SCHOCK, A TINY, mighty gal from Baltimore has influenced this six-foot-tall chick from across the country in all the best ways. While our stories are vastly different, her impact on me has loomed large. Learning about Gina's early start in punk rock and her vision for her band gave me the confidence to fiercely push my own female punk rock band to achieve everything we could. The hooks Gina brought to the Go-Go's songs informed my playing and still do.

The first surf song I ever saw played live was in 1981 when the Go-Go's played "Surfing and Spying." That performance hugely influenced my love of surf music, the music I have now played for decades with the Neptunas. The way Gina pours herself into every song and performance pushes me to employ my own brute, physical force when I play drums. Gina's desire to have a blast, combined with her tough work ethic and openness to allowing drum parts to evolve organically, have all contributed to my evolution as a drummer. I play drums with the sole purpose of making people feel great because that's how Gina makes me feel when I see her play. She works her ass off to bring the beat, and I strive to do the same. Just feeling the song and giving it what it needs—nothing more, nothing less.

I met Gina at a show she played at a club in Orange County, California, in the mid-nineties. I watched her play from behind the stage so I could see everything she did up close. It was really mind blowing, but even better was talking with her after the set. I told her that I play in an all-girl surf band and that I'm hugely inspired by her. She was incredibly humble.

She asked me, "Are ya havin' fun?"

My answer was, and remains, "Yes, Gina. I sure am."

Laura Bethita Neptuna *is a member of the Southern California female surf/garage/punk trio, the Neptunas. Laura played drums and contributed vocals on many of the Neptunas releases over the last two decades including two full length releases,* Mermaid A Go Go *(on Altered State of Reverb) and* Let Them Eat Tuna *(on Sympathy For the Record Industry).*

TOP FIVE FAVORITE PUNK DRUMMERS

By Pete Finestone

I NEVER REALLY PLANNED on playing the drums. When I was fifteen, my parents, desperately trying to find some direction for my directionless teenage life, suggested I try playing snare drum for my private school orchestra. I joined claiming I could play rudiments. At my first and only practice, the school director led the band in and, being the joker I was, I recklessly banged on the snare drum without a clue what the charts were. For the next six months, I proceeded to waste my parents' hard-earned money, taking lessons but never bothering to practice.

That soon ended and I never planned on picking up sticks and wasting anybody's time again. Then one night I had the opportunity to go see a Jethro Tull concert or the Clash at the Santa Monica Civic Auditorium. As fate had it, I picked the latter and that decision forever changed the direction of my life. I became a convert to this new force, this new music, this new language that had always been inside me, but I had never been able to access. I befriended the guys in Bad Religion soon after. We were all from the San Fernando Valley and I had a car, so Greg Graffin and I soon began our weekly Tuesday night jaunts to the Starwood to see the best punk bands from all over LA and its sprawling suburbs. I became their drummer's roadie and a confidant of the band. After Jay Ziskrout got canned, they asked me to take over the throne. It's a spot I occupied off and on from 1981 until 1992.

Here are five punk drummers who inspired me along the way.

Chuck Biscuits
D.O.A.

It's not even close. D.O.A. was a juggernaut from its inception. I remember getting in to see them for my first time and being able to get backstage. I noticed a big contingent of fans watching from behind the drummer, which was an anomaly. I soon joined that group and watched the entire set while having my head blown off by the young prodigy, Chuck Biscuits. What John Bonham was to rock, Biscuits was to punk. He might have been eighteen, but he pulled off these flam kick patterns with the aplomb of a vet, all while banging his head with a vengeance. From *Something Better Change* to the rest of his catalog with the band, he could play punk to reggae to rock effortlessly. I would put that lineup, with Randy Rampage on bass, against any punk band of the last forty-two years and say, "Good fucking luck keeping up." "Ya, hey!"

Topper Headon
The Clash

Could have easily been my top pick since he basically led the attack for the band that changed my damn life. Shit, where do you start with this man who could also play guitar and piano, and was responsible for cowriting one of the band's biggest hits ("Rock the Casbah")? Seeing him command the stage with his shiny Pearl kit, looking the part with black gloves and impeccable style, he could destroy you with "Tommy Gun" or have you swaying with "Straight to Hell." Like many of the greats, Top was well versed in many genres—maybe even more than Chuck Biscuits—and could dominate all the different styles the Clash demanded.

Lucky Lehrer
Circle Jerks

"Red tape, I can see, Can't you see?" How many drummers, trying to make it to the big dance, tried to replicate Lucky's ridiculous performance from "Red Tape"? I never did, since I knew few could. The man was playing on a four-piece, oversized Slingerland kit and it sounded like he was playing on Terry Bozzio's twenty-piece kit. Lucky was well-versed at the jazz and Latin game and on *Group Sex*—one of the greatest debuts from any band—he creatively snuck in single and double paradiddles (on songs like "Back Against the Wall") throughout that fifteen-minute masterpiece. Though the greatness of *Group Sex* was never matched, it left its mark on me and thousands of others.

Bobby Schayer
Bad Religion

"Like a rock, Like a planet, Like a fucking atom bomb." And so it began. The next phase after I prematurely left Bad Religion started with a couplet, rhythmically supported by a solo sixteenth note kick pattern that I dare you to try. Bobby Schayer was his name and you better fucking take notice. The album *Generator* was a hard one for me to swallow because, in no uncertain terms, I knew my old band had found a savant who never needed a double bass set up or more than four drums to let you know he had a pocket as deep as any canyon. Schayer could play with the attack of Keith Moon and swing like Charlie Watts. The band was in great hands and this sweet, talented man is still my friend to this day.

Charlie "Chalo" Quintana
The Plugz/Social Distortion

Chalo came to notoriety while playing for the great LA band the Plugz. I first saw them when they opened for P.I.L. at the Olympic Auditorium. A preternatural talent who went on to play with musical greats like Bob Dylan, he was another player with a style that matched his unwavering greatness behind the kit. After years of playing as a hired gun, he went on to helm the drums for Social Distortion during their most prolific decade. His pocket was as wide as his childhood's "Rio Grande," and, if you listened closely, you could instantly recognize his sound on any track he played on. RIP, my old friend. I hope you are somewhere in the sweet hereafter with a cig in mouth, pounding out your indelible sound.

Pete Finestone *played drums for seminal LA punk band Bad Religion from 1982 to 1992. He played on* Suffer, No Control, *and* Against The Grain, *three classics later memorialized as the "Holy Trinity." His playing helped define punk drumming for the next decade and inspired drummers from Pennywise to Blink-182.*

"How many drummers...tried to replicate **Lucky Lehrer**'s ridiculous performance from 'Red Tape'? I never did, since I knew few could." — Pete Finestone

Photo by Alison Braun, author of In The Pit-Photography by Alison Braun 1981-1990. *AlisonBraun.com*

"**Reed Mullin** was an "an intense and
gut-wrenching drummer boy."
—Hudley Flipside
Photo courtesy of ZUMA Press

"We all know **Travis Barker** is 'punk as fuck'… He's my ultimate drumming hero." —Shari Page

Photo courtesy of Abaca Press

"Everybody takes the bit they like best and presents it as the thing punk was built on. But the truth is it was built on sand, it was built on absolutely nothing."
—**Rat Scabies** (front)

Photo courtesy of Trinity Mirror

"I don't just think that **Brooks Wackerman** is the best to have played with [Bad Religion]—I think he's the best in the history of punk rock." —Ian Winwood

Photo courtesy of ZUMA Press

"**Dale Crover** is such a great guy and he's a great drummer. He's such a fan of music and that really comes through in his playing." —Steven McDonald

Photo courtesy of Gonzales Photo

"I've always thought of **Gina Schock** as a warrior." —Laura Bethita Neptuna

Photo courtesy of MediaPunch, Inc.

"I knew exactly what I wanted to do in life. There was never any 'Cover your bases. Learn a trade.' Fuck that. Just play drums." —**Tré Cool**

Photo courtesy of Gonzales Photo

"Playing with Bob [Mould] is like running a 10k while also being in a boxing match."
—Jon Wurster

Photo courtesy of Jon Wurster

"Praising **Derrick Plourde** as a punk drummer is selling him short.
His drumming and influences were diverse." —Joey Cape

Photo courtesy of Joey Cape

"I spent many days locked in my darkened room with a hand me down Discman and those practice pads..." —**Urian Hackney**
Photo courtesy of The Former Co.

"I guess, if I think back, I've always liked hitting stuff." —**Benny Horowitz**
Photo courtesy of Simon Newbury

"I'd watch the singer and guitar player, but I couldn't take my eyes off the drummer—to me that was the coolest thing I'd ever seen." —**Lori Barbero**

Photo courtesy of WEBB Rights Ltd.

"I learned from watching the drummers
from every band we toured with.
Style, tricks, equipment preference."
—**Phanie Diaz**

Photo courtesy of Phanie Diaz

"**Bill Stevenson**'s philosophy of drumming boils down to two things: speed
and consistency." —Jim Ruland

Photo by Alison Braun. AlisonBraun.com

"In other bands, the drummers typically twiddle their thumbs while waiting for the guitarist and the bass player to work it out. Not me." —**D. H. Peligro**

Photo courtesy of Clinton Wallace/ZUMA Press, Inc.

"I realized playing punk music meant expressing yourself however you wanted to; playing even if you didn't know how." —**Lynn Perko-Truell**

Photo courtesy of Lynn Perko-Truell

"When **Chuck Biscuits** was thirteen, he'd drum along with us on the bongos...
Little did we know he was going to turn into a punk rock phenom." —Joey Shithead

Photo by Alison Braun. AlisonBraun.com

JAN RADDER ON GRANT HART

Interviewed by S. W. Lauden

J AN RADDER WAS A fifteen-year-old punk rock and horror movie fan when he first worked with director and screenwriter Gorman Bechard as a production assistant on the cult-favorite *Psychos in Love*. After working on a few other eighties B-movies, he next collaborated with Bechard in 2009 when they coproduced the Replacements documentary, *Color Me Obsessed*. After interviewing the legendary Hüsker Dü drummer/songwriter/singer Grant Hart for that film, they decided to make him the subject of their next documentary, *Every Everything: The Music, Life & Times of Grant Hart*, which Radder coproduced and cowrote. It was released in 2013.

When did you personally first discover Hüsker Dü?

It was the fall of 1985 and I was a sophomore in high school. My friend, Matt, had just bought SST's *The Blasting Concept* the day before and I was getting ready to head off to our high school's Saturday football game because I played clarinet in the marching band. We were going to play at half-time and as the pep band. Matt called me almost in a panic as I was putting on my uniform. "Dude," he said, "you have GOT to hear this. It's this band Hüsker Dü." Neither of us had any idea how to pronounce the name right so when he said it, it came out HUSKER like maybe the band was influenced by Nebraska's Corn Huskers. I heard him drop the needle on his record player and then "Real World" came pounding out over the phone line. I sat there, in my bedroom, half of my band uniform on and the other half lying on my bed, listening to something that sounded like nothing I'd ever heard before. After we got off the phone, I finished getting dressed and then my mom drove me to the high school where I got on a bus to go to the game.

On the bus, I put on my headphones and tried to listen the Ramones' *Leave Home* on my Walkman but all I could think of was that trebly, high-pitched, distorted guitar, that almost droning bass, those drums that sounded almost like they were tripping over themselves, barely keeping upright as they pulsed and pounded and ran along the beat, and those melodic backing vocals. (Melodic? In punk? Seriously?) It's all I thought of on the bus ride, as we played Stravinsky's "Firebird," as we watched the football team lose yet another game, as we packed up to leave, and as we headed back home. I remember trying to tell someone else about this band, Hüsker Dü, that I'd just heard, and he was just like *Husker what?*

Thinking about the song, I imagined this group of skinny, angry young punks, dressed in leather and combat boots with buzz cuts who were ready to kick ass and take names. Two days later I happened to see them on IRS's *The Cutting Edge* promoting their new single, "Makes No Sense at All." I still remember feeling stunned when I saw them: a pudgy guy who looked like he might work down the street at the gas station, a long-haired hippie, and one of the guys from the Village People. Which only made them cooler. I mean, they looked like normal guys, maybe even dorks, but the sound they made was really like nothing I'd ever heard before. I was instantly hooked. To me, Hüsker Dü was making, by no stretch of the imagination, the best music of my generation regardless of whether the kids at school who called me a fag and a freak just because I didn't listen to Def Leppard or Journey knew it or not.

What's your favorite Hüsker Dü album?

It's really hard to pick one, and my favorite changes constantly. One day it might be *Zen Arcade* or *New Day Rising*. Another it might be *Metal Circus* or *Flip Your Wig*. As far as drumming, though I knew Grant was the drummer, it wasn't what he did on a kit that first hit me. It was his songwriting and singing. The anguish of "Diane," the pop melodicism of "Pink Turns to Blue," the passion of "Keep Hanging On." Black Flag might have the rage, Minutemen might have the art punk groove, Descendents might have the pop-punk melody, but no one except Hüsker Dü could put all of it together into one coherent sound and song. To me, they were like the Beatles.

As a punk musician yourself, what was it like to work with one of your musical heroes?

Honestly, it really was a dream come true. There were so many times I thought to myself, if I could go back in time and talk to my fifteen-year-old self and tell him that one day he'd be making a film with Grant Hart, he'd tell me I was full of shit. The first song I ever wrote was me trying to sound like Grant. The reason I moved to Minneapolis from Connecticut was because of Hüsker Dü. When I was playing in punk bands in the late eighties and early nineties, all we wanted to do, just like pretty much every other band around, was to sound like them. It's not often that we get to meet our idols in real life let alone make a film with them.

One of my favorite things about the documentary is how much it's driven by Grant Hart himself. What was it like to work with him?

Grant was one of the most creative and brilliant people I've met, and pretty damn funny to boot. While he had a hands-off approach to the film, there were definitely touches he added. For instance, if you've seen the film, you've noticed the outfit he wore, namely the coat. That was his nod to Robert McNamara, who wore something similar for the poster of *Fog of War*. Grant came to the set every day wearing that coat, his pink shirt, the suspenders, his red shoes and jeans, and his hair pomaded back. He called it his "McNamara drag" (he even suggested an ending where he finally takes off his McNamara drag, puts on his motorcycle jacket, and walks off into the sunset).

The most magical moment, though, the one that gave us all goosebumps when he did it, was the tour of his no-longer-there home. In leading up to the shooting, I'd reached out to Grant to find out if there were any specific places he wanted to film at. One of the things we did was find locations that were important to Grant as touchstones, moments, or just places he was connected to. I then took our interview questions and paired them with the location so that they would fit the connection Grant had to the place. For instance, when we filmed him at the former site of Cheapo Records where he first met Bob Mould, our questions were all about the early history of Hüsker Dü. Talking to Grant, he threw out a couple of suggestions and then asked me what sorts of things we were looking for from him. I told him that one of the things we were thinking about was trying to do something similar to what the filmmakers who made *We Jam Econo* did with Mike Watt. In that film, Watt took the filmmakers on a tour of his old neighborhood in his tour van, which he's incredibly proud of and feels an innate connection to, pointing out where he'd first met D. Boon, where he first saw a bass guitar, where the Minutemen played their first gig, and things like that. I said to Grant that we were hoping to do something similar when we interviewed him in South St. Paul [where he grew up] and at the site of his old home but not copy it. Grant said he'd think about it.

When we got to the day where we visited his old home (which, by then, was only a newly seeded grassy field), we started setting up for the shoot. Our plan was to ask Grant questions about his family, his childhood, and what happened to the house. As we set up, Grant picked up a branch from the ground and paced around. When we finished, Grant said, "Are you all set?" "Yep," we said. "Is the film rolling?" "Yep." "The sound?" "Yep." "…Come on in," he said, and went into the spiel that you see at the start of the film. He then took us on a tour of his no-longer-in-existence home, giving directions to watch out for steps and things that might fall over, telling us he's going to get around to cleaning up the mess, calling out to his mother who had stepped out for a moment, and taking us through every single room in his home and bringing to life this place that was no longer there. It was absolutely brilliant and so completely Grant. When he finished, I'm pretty sure all of our mouths were hanging open, and then Gorman says, "Grant, that was incredible. Can you do it again?" He was worried that because we didn't have a lavalier on Grant the sound might not be all that great. Grant protested and then finally agreed, but he was super pissed. His opening for the second take was pretty sarcastic and flippant but as he went through the tour, he got into what he was doing again. We wound up using a mix of both takes in the film. As soon as we saw that first tour, though, we knew we had our opening for the film. And as we edited the movie, we realized that the tour also provided the framework for our story where we'd go from story to story and idea to idea before eventually winding up back where we began, standing outside Grant's house at the very end of the film. Which was a lot like having a conversation with Grant. You'd ask him a question and he'd start to answer it and then go off on a tangent and then another tangent and then maybe a third tangent and eventually he would bring all of the tangents together as he answered the question you'd originally asked. If there's any moment in *Every Everything* that captures Grant best, it's that tour of the house. I'm just glad we were able to capture it.

In addition to drumming and singing in Hüsker Dü, he also designed all of the album covers. How do you think his artist's brain influenced his unique approach to drumming?

Grant was a person who seemed to have a million things going on creatively inside his brain at the same time. He was always thinking and noticing and picking up on those chance encounters that create a lasting image or sound. In the film, Grant talks about working on Studebakers and model airplanes as the mathematical accuracy that he often neglected in other areas. I think, in some ways, you could say that was what his drumming was. On the surface it seems almost chaotic and out of control, sort of how Keith Moon's drumming was. But beneath that seeming chaos there was a system and a beat that held everything down. It was the mathematical backing to each of the songs he played that held everything else together like glue. The music might seem like it's going in a million different directions but really it's all being held in place and has an internal logic to it. In many ways, you can say that's similar to his album art. That each artwork is confined by the dimensions of an album cover is similar to the confines of his drumming. There is a beat and a time and measure that holds everything in place, just as the 12x12 square of a record cover holds its art in place.

How did your opinion of his drumming evolve while making the film?

As we made the film and as I watched more and more footage of Grant drumming and listened more and more carefully to what he was playing, I gained even more respect for what he was doing. So often, it sounded like Grant's drumming was almost out of control, like it was about to split apart from the song but had to be held in place by the Bob's guitar and Greg's bass, much like Keith Moon's drumming was a lead instrument held together by Entwistle's bass. The more I listened closely, though, the more I heard how Grant created the illusion of being out of control, of surfing on top of the sonic landscape created by Bob's guitar when it was really Grant who was holding everything together, a master illusionist who hid the strings and hidden doors so well that no one who wasn't really paying close attention would notice.

Gene Krupa, Keith Moon, and Ringo Starr are among the influences he names in the film. Are there any modern drummers who you think are obviously influenced by Grant Hart?

That's a really good question. I don't know if there are any. I know that Dave Grohl is very influenced by Hüsker Dü, but I don't hear Grant in his drumming…. One thing I can say is that there seem to be few drummers who create a sound that is so uniquely theirs that the moment you hear them you know who they are and that they stand out almost as a lead instrument while still keeping time and providing a backbone for every song they play on. George Hurley of the Minutemen is certainly one. Keith Moon, Ringo

Starr, and Gene Krupa, while not an exhaustive list, are others. I think you could for sure include Grant on that list as well.

If you haven't, check out his drumming on the last album he played on, Yanomamos' *Comes Alive*. He recorded the first side before his cancer diagnosis and the second side in early 2017 when he was really starting to feel poorly, but it's the second-side drumming that really outshines the first—where you hear him playing things that, on one hand, sound so unlike anything he'd played in the past, but on the other hand sound so uniquely like Grant. And when you hear it, you realize what a truly unique treasure Grant was.

BILL STEVENSON: A CONSISTENCY OF PRESSURE

By Jim Ruland

BILL STEVENSON WAS A fidgety kid who loved to fish.
From an early age he banged on things—pots and pans at home and notebooks at school—until his father broke down and bought him a snare drum. Stevenson pounded away, imitating the martial beats of the marching band at school, but he had no interest in joining them.

"I never wanted to be in a school band," Stevenson said. "I didn't think I was qualified so I never looked into it. I didn't have any connection to school or teams or clubs or anything. I just wasn't part of that."

Stevenson attended Mira Costa High School in Manhattan Beach, the incubator of Southern California punk rock luminaries like Greg Ginn of Black Flag and Jim Lindberg of Pennywise. Stevenson's introduction to punk rock came not from his friends at school but through fishing. Stevenson was a regular customer at the Hermosa Tackle Box where he bought his equipment and bait. The Tackle Box was owned by Jerry Morris, whose son Keith was the vocalist of a band called Panic! that would soon change its name to Black Flag.

"By the time I was about thirteen," Stevenson explained, "I was kind of known as a pretty good fishing rod builder. So, I started building rods and finishing them and then bringing them to Keith's dad and selling them at Jerry's Tackle Box."

Jerry was so impressed with Stevenson's fishing rods that he hired him to build them in the shop where he had a machine that allowed him to work on several at a time and speed up the process. "Keith and I spent a lot of time back there in that unventilated back room, inhaling the fumes of the fishing rod finish," Stevenson said. "I feel like that probably didn't do my brain cells any good being back there all that time. But we'd sit back there, and Keith would tell me about bands to check out. He was the first person that told me about the Stooges."

Meanwhile, Stevenson's snare had expanded into a full drum set. The guy who sold it to him taught Stevenson two basic beats: a rock beat and a Latin beat. That three-minute lesson was the only musical instruction he ever received. Before long, he was playing along to his favorite records: KISS, Aerosmith, Ted Nugent, Black Sabbath, and the Rolling Stones.

Stevenson's friend and classmate Dave Nolte was trying to get Stevenson into punk rock, but not having much luck. He gave him tapes to listen to, but Stevenson didn't like any of it except Devo's "Mongoloid," which he loved.

Greg Ginn had invited Dave and his older brother Joe to the space where Panic! rehearsed. (Joe sang and played guitar in the Last, the only other punk band in Hermosa Beach at the time.) The Nolte brothers brought Stevenson along, and after practice, a jam session broke out. Stevenson learned the Devo tune and played some Black Sabbath songs, but the session took an unexpected turn when they started playing original music, which was a life-altering experience for him. "You mean people like us can come up with riffs?" Stevenson remembered thinking. "Wow, that is fantastic. I want to try to get into this."

Not only was it the first time Stevenson had played with other people, it was also his first exposure to mind-altering substances, but he didn't partake. Stevenson was a fisherman, and fishermen get up early. His drug of choice—then and now—was coffee. "I was a young little kid just kind of mesmerized to be there. Plus, I had never been to a party before. This was a party where there were people drinking and smoking dope and stuff. I had never seen that before. I was a very naive little boy."

This heady experience encouraged Stevenson to keep jamming with Dave and writing songs, which he discovered he had a knack for. "I couldn't have had the drum set for more than five months and then we started the Descendents," Stevenson said. "So, I barely knew how to play. None of us did."

Dave had been writing material with Frank Navetta, who shared Stevenson's passion for fishing, but Dave left the band to play in the Last with his brother Joe. Stevenson and Frank were joined by bassist Tony Lombardo, and they recorded a single at Media Art, the recording studio where Black Flag recorded their first two EPs. That record caught the attention of classmate Milo Auckerman, who joined the band as the Descendents vocalist.

The Descendents' rehearsals were powered by a juddering concoction called the "Bonus Cup," which was achieved by filling a coffee mug a third of the way with instant coffee, five blasts of sugar, and boiling water. Driven by caffeine-fueled beats, the Descendents combined the hardcore of Black Flag with the pop sensibilities of the Last, creating a lightning-fast blend that was catchy and crude. The Descendents first EP, *Fat*, was released on New Alliance Records, the San Pedro-based label founded by D. Boon and Mike Watt of the Minutemen. Stevenson cowrote two of the band's earliest songs, "I Like Food" and "Wienerschnitzel"— each approximately ten seconds long.

The Descendents followed up *Fat* with the groundbreaking *Milo Goes to College*, fifteen songs of teenage fury that established the band as unlikely progenitors of melodic hardcore. Stevenson even managed to sneak in a song about running out of gas on a fishing trip to Catalina. But the band lost steam when Milo left to attend college. The remaining members tried to keep the project going for a while. Stevenson was still in high school when he got a call from his friends in Black Flag. The band's drummer, Robo, had been detained in London due to immigration issues. They wanted to know if Stevenson could fly out to New York and fill in. Stevenson said, "Let me ask my dad."

Within a matter of minutes, Stevenson was on his way to the airport to meet up with Black Flag, who were touring with Saccharine Trust, another band from LA's South Bay. Stevenson showed up at the infamous Mudd Club in New York in the middle of winter—without a coat. He shrugged off the cold and went to work. "I was all set to help out my friends and do my best to make Robo proud of me," Stevenson said.

Aside from playing the occasional song too fast, the rest of the tour went off without a hitch. "I got to just sit there and drink my coffee and watch Saccharine Trust play before we did," Stevenson recalled. "It was like, 'Man, life doesn't get any better than this!'"

It didn't happen right away, but eventually the fill-in gig turned full-time. Stevenson joined Black Flag when the band was ramping up its touring operation and recording schedule. Stevenson played on the albums *My War, Family Man, Slip It In, Loose Nut*, and *In My Head*, and on the EPs *TV Party* and *The Process of Weeding Out*.

The hardest parts for Stevenson weren't the grueling months on the road or the all-night recording sessions, but simply slowing down his drumming. Stevenson joined Black Flag at a time when the band was turning away from hardcore punk and exploring a darker, heavier sound that became increasingly experimental with each subsequent album. "There were definitely some awkward growing pains there," Stevenson said.

He adapted his playing style from the ultra-fast hardcore songs of early Black Flag to the metallic sludge of *My War*'s side two, to the jazz-fusion freak outs of the instrumental albums. "I wasn't ever really great at playing slow," Stevenson said. His favorite songs to play were "Police Story," "Jealous Again," "Depression," and "American Waste," all written before he joined the band.

Stevenson left Black Flag in 1985 and rejoined the Descendents. They recorded three more albums—*I Don't Want to Grow Up, Enjoy,* and *All*—after which Auckerman left the band again. This prompted Stevenson to form the band All with the remaining members, and they cranked out a steady stream of records.

When punk rock went mainstream in 1994 with bands like Green Day, Offspring, and Rancid climbing to the top of the charts, the Descendents finally started to receive the recognition it deserved for being pop-punk pioneers who, along with bands like Bad Religion, paved the way for the next generation of punk rockers. That year, Stevenson built a professional recording studio in Fort Collins, Colorado, with his bandmates in All. In addition to recording scores of bands, including Good Riddance, Rise Against, and Propagandhi, Stevenson continued to play, writing new music for All and the Descendents. In 2004, he started the band Only Crime and even played drums for the Lemonheads.

Widely regarded as the fastest right hand in punk, Stevenson insists that's no longer the case. "The older I get the harder it is to keep up that tempo," he said. After battling some serious health issues that would have sidelined most people, including having a brain tumor removed and open-heart surgery, Stevenson now incorporates yoga and stretching into his preshow routine. The one-time aficionado of Wienerschnitzel has upped his broccoli consumption to keep his body in better condition.

Growing older and wiser has also impacted his coffee intake. "I have to drink a whole thermos full of espresso, not coffee but espresso," Stevenson said. In order to get the kick Stevenson needs to play those early Descendents songs, he has to increase his coffee consumption when he's playing a show, and then wean himself off it again when the tour's over.

"I try to deprive myself of coffee when I don't have a show," Stevenson said. "So, let's say, on a just normal daily basis, I'll try to limit it to like, two cups. Because if you keep it up to ten cups every day, then pretty soon ten cups becomes no cups."

Stevenson's philosophy of drumming boils down to two things: speed and consistency. "There's just a certain velocity at which the drums sound good. I wouldn't call it hard or soft, I would call it consistent. Because if you hit them too hard, you choke the tone out of them, they just sound brittle. So, it's more like a consistency of pressure, as opposed to erratic flailing around."

For those just starting out and thinking about modeling their style off of his drumming, Stevenson has just one word of advice: don't.

"Just be true to your heart and play things that make your heart feel good and make you feel like you're expressing your true personality. You're not imitating anyone and you're not doing it to get famous. You're not doing it to get rich. You're not doing it to attract companionship. You're doing it because you love it because the music makes you feel good inside. That's it."

That and a lot of coffee.

Jim Ruland *is the coauthor of* My Damage *with Keith Morris and* Do What You Want *with Bad Religion. His book* Corporate Rock Sucks: The Rise and Fall of SST Records *will be published in the spring of 2022.*

DC WILL DO THAT TO YOU

By Eric Beetner

THE MOST FORMATIVE PERIOD in my musical awakening happened when I spent a few weeks in Washington, DC, with my aunt and uncle. My older cousins, high schoolers at the time, introduced a twelve-year-old me to Devo, the Romantics, Elvis Costello, the B-52s, Kraftwerk and obscure local bands like Tiny Desk Unit. I came home to Connecticut transformed.

That new-wave indoctrination quickly led to my discovery of hardcore punk and DC bands were among the first I noticed. That region has loomed so large ever since that it's common for me to say all my favorite bands come from Washington, DC.

What does any young teenager latch onto with hardcore? Yes, the screaming vocals speak to our hearts, but the shock of electricity that shoots from our cerebellum down to the base of our spine comes from the drumming. When I first heard the M-16 pounding of Jeff Nelson on Minor Threat's *First Two 7"* LP, only the second hardcore record I ever owned, I was a convert for life.

In Connecticut, I was in the corridor between New York and Boston, two hardcore scenes with their Doc Marten's firmly planted on their own ground and unwilling to move. I lived thankfully close to a major club, the Anthrax, which got national touring acts. All the biggest and best bands came through town, so I could see them without having to hop a train into NYC for a show at CBGB, though I did make it to a handful of shows there in the mid-eighties. So, I saw a cross-section of bands from all over the US playing what had by 1984 become a set genre of music. The burst of speed, then the slower moshing part and the shout-along chorus—it had all become cliché in only a few short years until you could scarcely tell the difference between a touring band or a local band. I had little defense when my friends (*not* hardcore fans at all) complained that all the music sounded the same in my endless attempts at jamming a cassette into a car stereo and trying to get them to understand the subtle differences between DYS from Boston and DRI from Texas.

But DC was different. They had their own thing. A small scene, cordial and supportive, driven by bands all chasing that elusive sound laid down by Bad Brains and imitated by drummers all trying to keep up with Earl Hudson. They also had Dischord Records, which made the DC scene so easy to follow. I was too young to ever have seen Minor Threat or S.O.A. (Henry Rollins' band before Black Flag, who were equally as powerful) and could never make it to a show at the 9:30 Club or DC Space, so I missed out on the advantages of being a local in any hardcore scene. But thankfully, tracing the DC scene from afar was as simple as keeping up with the Dischord catalog.

When Minor Threat broke up, I followed the members everywhere they scattered, always waiting for Jeff Nelson to pop up in another band and instantly buying, unheard, any album with his name on it. I'll admit, though, that High Back Chairs were no Minor Threat 2.0. Bands like Government Issue, Swiz, Black Market Babies, VOID, and Youth Brigade all had vinyl lined up on my shelf, all driven by powerful drum sounds expertly captured at Inner Ear Studios by Don Zientara, a man who knew how to record hardcore drums as well as anyone. Most hardcore drumming fell into two categories back then: sloppy or tight. DC bands were capital "T" Tight.

DC moved away from lock-step hardcore pretty quickly, and I followed with glee. In defiance of some punk aesthetics, the bands seemed to want to get better at their instruments and nowhere was this more apparent than with the drumming. Enter Brendan Canty of Fugazi. His off-kilter rhythms changed the game and defined post-punk, helping to inspire (dare I say it) more bands than even Minor Threat.

And then he brought out that bell! You'd see it next to his kit before the band played like Chekov's gun up there, waiting for the moment when he reached over mid-song to clang the huge thing, and it rang out through whatever room they were playing without ever being mic'd. Ringing a big-ass bell is the most un-punk thing and yet somehow the most punk thing in the world. The other element Fugazi introduced was silence. The well-placed pause in a song that hit as hard as a tightly wound snare. The bands out of New York and Boston would never think to stop and give the listener time to think like that.

I finally got my chance to see Bad Brains live on the *I Against I* tour. One of the most amazing moments of any show I ever saw was when they switched effortlessly from the most brutal hardcore assault out there into a reggae tune, and Earl kept a room full of sweaty suburban kids moving like we'd all just teleported to a dancehall in Jamaica.

But the bands that ended up speaking to me the loudest, and who I still name on my list of favorites, were many of those post-punk DC bands. Shudder to Think, Jawbox, Fugazi, the Dismemberment Plan, Smart Went Crazy (the title of this essay was taken from a pair of songs from their brilliant album *Con Art*). They were still tethered to the expectations of the Dischord label, but the drummers seemed to want to stretch the limits of what a punk band could sound like. New terms like "math rock" were invented just to keep up with the acrobatic time changes of the drummers, most of whom seemed to come from the DC area.

I didn't think it could get any better than Shudder to Think's *Get Your Goat* LP or Jawbox's *Novelty*. Then Mike Russell announced he and guitarist Chris Matthews were leaving Shudder, and I figured it was over. But wait! In steps Adam Wade from Jawbox to take over and Zach Barocas moves into his seat in Jawbox and it leads to career-best records from both bands— Shudder's *Pony Express Record* and Jawbox's *For Your Own Special Sweetheart*. Was there a bad or even mediocre drummer in the entire DC metro area?

Years later, I got to see a reformed Jawbox play a show where Shudder to Think's Craig Wedren was the opening act. From the stage, he publicly apologized for the first time for "stealing their drummer." Adam Wade was also in the crowd and it was clear there was no animosity. DC is like that. You can poach someone's world-class drummer and no hard feelings. Can you imagine in LA if Guns 'N Roses had stolen Jane's Addiction's drummer? Fistfights and broken bottles of Jack Daniel's all around!

We all know the story of a young Dave Grohl being picked up by DC outfit Scream as their replacement drummer. Being the second or third guy in the seat seemed to be the sweet spot.

The drummers of the DC scene were always more than just the guys who sat behind the kit. Jeff Nelson was also a talented artist who defined the look of the early Dischord releases and created the iconic black sheep, which, if my wife would let me, I would have tattooed on my body right now.

Ryan Nelson, drummer for the Most Secret Method, is also a talented visual artist for his own band and others. Smart Went Crazy drummer, Devin Ocampo, played such complex rhythms that I assumed he was some Berklee-trained savant on the kit, only to follow him on to his next band, Faraquet, and discover him playing guitar brilliantly. Then onto his next band, Medications, where he did the same. He's the Dave Grohl-style drummer-guitarist-singer you *don't* know about.

Shudder to Think was the band I'd seen live more than any other, until the Dismemberment Plan came along. Joe Easley is one of those drummers so quietly brilliant that you can't believe he's not a household name. Always there with the perfect fill, never overplaying but always offering something interesting, and I can replicate those beats perfectly with my index fingers on my steering wheel to this day. I've had years of practice.

The best of the DC sound is defined by the drums that are a cut above. Any healthy music scene feeds off of and inspires itself. Whether it's competition, being inspired by seeing a band play, or having a supportive community that encourages experimentation and stretching, DC had a special magic that continues to this day.

There's a reason armies follow drummers into battle. They draw us to them. I've been chasing that sound ever since I first stared at that drawing of the Capitol dome being struck by lightning—you know the one—and heard the relentless crack of the snare drum that went with it, the sound of the energy and electricity in that image. Once the DC sound shook my spine, I've never been the same. DC will do that to you.

Eric Beetner *is author of over two dozen crime novels. He was guitarist / vocalist for post-punk bands* Go! Dog! Go! *and* Build Your Own Monster—*bands people did not like. By the time he left high school, he'd seen over two hundred punk/hardcore bands and already had hearing damage.*

TOP FIVE PUNK(ISH) SONGS TO MAKE YOU A BETTER DRUMMER

By Jon Wurster

I GUESS YOU COULD say I've had an on-again, off-again relationship with punk rock drumming.

When I was thirteen, a year after I got my first drum kit, I pretty much ditched my classic rock albums and began drumming along to punk and new-wave records by the Ramones, the Clash, the Police, and the Pretenders. The Southeastern Pennsylvania-based bands I played with in the early- and mid-eighties were all punk-adjacent, sharing stages with the likes of the Minutemen, Suicidal Tendencies, and Die Kreuzen. So, I was pretty entrenched in that world by early eighty-six, when I decided to audition for, and ultimately joined, a major label-bound North Carolina-roots rock band called the Right Profile.

Even though the Right Profile was named after a Clash song, its members were hardcore Rolling Stones, Bob Dylan and the Band fans, so it was a very different scene for me, drumming-wise. I was a Dylan and Stones fan when I was a kid but had never played a song by either of them before I joined the band. I had to quickly refine and simplify my manic drumming style to serve the Right Profile's groove-oriented songs. I'm forever grateful for this because it gave me skills I've been able to use over the years when I've had the opportunity to work with artists like Aimee Mann, Nick Cave, Jay Farrar, and the Mountain Goats.

The Right Profile never got to finish our debut album for Arista Records (the usual label problems and red tape you've heard a million times), and the band eventually called it a day in the fall of ninety-one when I joined Chapel Hill indie punks Superchunk. By that point, I was much more of a traditional rock and roll drummer, and I needed to quickly get my punk-rock chops back before embarking on my first Superchunk tour. The band's previous drummer, Chuck Garrison, was fantastic at playing fast, super-tight snare rolls, and I really needed to work to get up to his level. In addition to learning Superchunk songs, I spent a lot of time playing along with records like D.O.A.'s *War on 45*, the Minutemen's live compilation *Ballot Result*, and the Descendents' *Milo Goes to College*.

Though I love classic, early-eighties thrash, I'm lucky none of the bands I play with have ever really touched on it. "Staying Home," Superchunk's lone foray into that world, had to be retired from live shows because I kept getting lost and couldn't find the "one." It's quite embarrassing, and I am in awe whenever I hear thrash drumming masters like Al Schvitz (Millions of Dead Cops), Reed Mullin (Corrosion of Conformity), Earl Hudson (Bad Brains), Jeff Nelson (Minor Threat), and Pat Doyle (the Offenders).

I've been beyond fortunate to have gotten to play drums with former-Hüsker Dü/Sugar singer/guitarist Bob Mould for the last eleven years. Playing with Bob is like running a 10k while also being in a boxing match. It's by far the most physically demanding thing I've ever done, and it doesn't get any easier as the years go by. So, what's a fifty-five-year-old boy to do when he has to get ready for a grueling tour? He plays along with a strength-building punk playlist, of course!

Okay, I realize only a couple of these songs can truly be considered capital-P "Punk." Nevertheless, they play a crucial role in getting me into fighting form:

"Holidays in the Sun"
Sex Pistols

I think *Never Mind the Bollocks, Here's The Sex Pistols* is the greatest rock and roll album of all-time, and Paul Cook's drumming on this tune is the blueprint for a lot of what I do in the Bob Mould Band. This song is perfect for getting good at playing powerfully, while not letting a fast song get out of control, tempo-wise. It's a balancing act that's not as easy as it sounds.

"G.I."
Government Issue

Marc Alberstadt is one of the most underrated punk drummers of all time, and this song is the ultimate master class in the kind of fast snare rolls I mentioned earlier. "G.I." is only forty-seconds long, but by the end of that second chorus, I'm usually yelling "Oh, fuck you, Marc!" as I throw my sticks across the room in self-disgust.

"Tattooed Love Boys"
The Pretenders

Incredibly, I got to play this surprisingly fast, musical math problem with its composer, Chrissie Hynde, when I filled in for drummer Martin Chambers at a one-off Pretenders show a few years ago. An article I found on the song says it's in 7/16 ("a time signature that is rarely found in any genre at any point in history"), but I would wager Chrissie didn't have that in mind when she was writing it. I think she just knew it sounded awesome. I had a couple months to prepare for the show and I don't think I've ever practiced a single song more than "Tattooed Love Boys." My goal was to have every second of the song in my muscle memory, so as to not screw it up on the night. And wouldn't you know, I DID screw it up at soundcheck. But, like most mistakes, it was a gift. I recovered immediately, which dissolved any fears I had of the song grinding to a halt and me being pelted with garbage. For the record, I played it right during the show, and I still practice it often to keep both my body and brain in shape.

"Swimming Ground"
Meat Puppets

Oh, my achin' wrist! I suppose most Ramones songs would serve the same purpose, but there's something about drummer Derrick Bostrom's subtly manic performance that makes this an unmitigated arm-destroyer. For decades, I assumed Bostrom played the song's ridiculously relentless hi-hat pattern with both hands, but early Meat Puppets YouTube footage reveals him to be using only one. And to that I say, nobody likes a show-off.

"We Got the Beat"
The Go-Go's

This is essentially "Swimming Ground," but for my leg. A lot of Bob Mould songs feature a constant, pumping bass drum, and I freely admit I was as bad at this when I began playing with Bob as I was at those fast snare rolls when I joined Superchunk. Gina Schock is one of my drumming heroes and her steady-yet-swinging performance here is what makes her one of the best in the business. If I can get through this calf-cramper without stopping to regroup, I know I'm ready to get in the van.

Jon Wurster *has been the drummer for indie-rock pioneers Superchunk for the last thirty years. In 2008, Wurster joined the acclaimed folk-rock band The Mountain Goats, and a year later started playing with punk/alternative rock legend Bob Mould. Wurster is an in-demand drummer, recording or playing live with artists like Chrissie Hynde, the New Pornographers, Nick Cave, Ben Gibbard, and Rocket from the Crypt.*

LORI BARBERO ON BABES IN TOYLAND

Interviewed by S. W. Lauden

L ORI BARBERO DISCOVERED PUNK rock as a teenager in late seventies New York before moving back to Minneapolis and becoming part of the legendary music scene at Jay's Longhorn Bar. She had never played an instrument before founding Babes in Toyland with Kat Bjelland in the mid-eighties, but was always drawn to the drums. Her self-taught, propulsive style and dedication to authenticity have been an inspiration for countless drummers ever since.

You experienced the seventies New York punk scene as a teen. How did you discover punk?

Yes, I went to high school in New York and ended up in New York City, because the hamlet I was living in a few miles away was a one-horse town. Me being the city girl, I had to check out where all the fun was happening. Ended up hanging out in the Village, probably one or two weekends a month. I think I just ended up at some club and grasped onto that and it was history from there. I would not be on the road I am now if I didn't have those experiences then. I think the show that stands out the most would be Patti Smith on New Year's Eve 1977. Bruce Springsteen jumped on stage and sang "Because the Night" with her.

Would you consider any NYC punk drummers to be early influences?

I always watch the drummer, since I was young and saw bands play at music festivals. Of course, I'd watch the singer and guitar player, but I couldn't take my eyes off the drummer—to me that was the coolest thing I'd ever seen. Clem Burke [Blondie], Marky Ramone [Ramones], Johnny Blitz [Dead Boys], and Jerry Nolan [New York Dolls, Heartbreakers] are the ones that come to mind. Such a high-powered period for music.

Is it true that you never played drums prior to forming Babes in Toyland with Kat Bjelland?

Babes in Toyland was the first band I ever played drums in. In fact, it was the first time I ever played drums... I never played any other instrument. I wanted to be the drummer because there weren't very many female drummers, and I wanted to try it out. Also, I just thought it was the coolest looking instrument to play.

Which drummers did you turn to for inspiration once you started playing?

My biggest influences were probably the first bands I saw where I kind of really got interested in watching how they performed. When I completely decided I wanted to play drums, there was a female drummer from the Minneapolis punk band NNB named Cindy Blum. She just impressed me so much that I figured, if she can do it, I can do it. Quite an inspiration, and I have given her credit since day one. So, playing drums alongside Kat Bjelland was pretty much my schooling. I'm self-taught, even though it was suggested a couple times maybe I'd take a few lessons—but I threw that idea in the big dumpster.

How has your approach to drumming changed over the years?

To be honest, I really don't know how my drumming has changed. I'm a tom-tom girl, very tribal. That inspiration, or the footprints I follow, were from Martin Atkins [PIL] and Tony Pucci [Man Sized Action]. Of course, Grant Hart [Hüsker Dü] was quite an inspiration also, including playing drums barefoot. I much prefer playing live because of the energy and it's just raw and in your face, just like Babes in Toyland.

Who are some of your favorite punk drummers or bands performing today?

Quite honestly, I think all drummers deserve a pat on the back no matter how experienced they are or what style they play. Just the idea of moving those SOBs is enough for an award. I've produced a few songs for a female punk rock band from San Antonio, Texas called Fea. They're on Blackheart Records, and they're really great. They did a few shows with us on our reunion tour. Skating Polly and Kitten Forever also supported us, as well. They all rule.

What advice would you give to a drummer who just joined their first punk band?

My only advice is stick with your heart and your intuition. You can't be concerned about what anyone else says, because you're never ever going to please everyone. Do what makes you happy and life will treat you well. I always said, "When it's not fun anymore, I'm done."

THE ANGRY BUILDER

By Joey Cape

T HE ONLY THING ABOUT Derrick Plourde that made him a
drummer was that he happened to play drums. Before music
became a full-time job, he was on his way to being a pro skater,
he could fix cars, play any instrument he picked up. He was
endlessly tinkering. In his spare time, he made furniture. He also
built our rehearsal studio from the ground up in his parents'
backyard. He came to be known by his childhood friends as "The
Angry Builder." Derrick was simply never satisfied. He had great
discipline and extraordinary focus. Meticulous in his approach,
he took notes and made lists. He never wanted to stop learning
and growing. It was more than ambition. It was an unparalleled
kind of dedication, so impressive that it warranted respect and
deserved success. Even in the later years of his life, he took
drum lessons.

I like to think some musicians are painters and others are
mathematicians. Derrick was neither or both, depending on how
you look at it. He was, at least, something different. The great
Keith Moon was always painting while hanging on by a thread.
He would insert a drum fill in the middle of bar one, and we
sometimes wondered where or when he was going to land. Other
drummers play with a kind of precision that feels safe, but they

lack vision and feel. They get the basic job done, but there is little mystery. Derrick's drumming ability and style were reflected by his great attention to detail, yet his drumming never seemed calculated. He always painted a big and small picture in the track. Praising Derrick Plourde as a punk drummer is selling him short. His drumming and influences were diverse. While most young music fans might hang a poster of some "rock god" on their bedroom wall, at age fifteen Derrick had a poster of Buddy Rich. His influences ranged from Richard "Bomber" Manzullo of RKL to Neil Peart of Rush, from Jeff Porcaro of Toto to Phil "Philthy Animal" Taylor of Motörhead. Derrick was a multifaceted drummer and for that reason he was influential to many.

Lagwagon's Chris Flippin (Flip) told me a great story. Flip recalled being backstage and overhearing a conversation between Derrick and a young Travis Barker. Barker praised Derrick's drumming and asked a few questions, something that always made Derrick uncomfortable. To Derrick, it was a waste of time just talking about things. His philosophy was more "just get it done." He asked Travis what music he listened to. Travis answered and Derrick didn't like the answer, so Derrick told Travis to be more sophisticated and broaden his influences. I doubt he used those words, but that's the gist of the story. I like to think Derrick had something to do with Travis becoming the great drummer he is today. I have heard so many drummers speak of Derrick as the catalyst for their approach.

When I first started making music with Derrick, he was an all-out maniac. He filled every break in the action and did it all on a four-piece kit. Yet, from the start, he had respect for the other musicians and their lines. He had color and flair, and, over time, he developed control. His ability to play to the song developed and flourished over the years, as well. A simple arrangement felt more progressive with Derrick adding to the intricacies, begging for evolution. A good hook or bridge set to his creative foundation had a deeper impact. Something any songwriter wants in a musician. Derrick had an enormous effect on my writing. He was a brave drummer and made me a braver songwriter. It never once felt out of control or boring to me. I always knew what he was thinking and where he was going. We were in sync. Music was a conversation and Derrick finished my sentences. A musical soulmate.

Derrick and I both strived to bring diverse influences to the band. Everyone in Lagwagon listened to many styles of music. A guest in our van was more likely to hear Steely Dan than Black Flag. But it was Derrick who set the foundation for Lagwagon's sound and his framework is still there.

The early years of Lagwagon were spent touring, almost constantly, playing 250 to 280 shows a year from 1992–1995. None of us paid rent because we were always on the road. It was great. Derrick thrived on tour. He welcomed the challenge of a nightly show and seemed at ease with the van travel, writing daily in his journals in silence. He was tough. I remember him breaking his wrist while skateboarding on a tour, but he didn't skip a show. He just taped it up and played through the pain. I could tell how much it hurt. It took a few more broken limbs for the band to wise up. We made a rule about "no board sports on tour," to which no one abided.

Derrick's drumming was outstanding live. His playing and confidence flourished on the road. Every night he had his own audience. People surrounded the kit and never looked away. I understood why. Nightly, he would do something back there that surprised even me. Several times in our set I would find myself thinking, "Why didn't he do that on the record?" He was tastefully experimental without losing the backbone we needed to deliver a great show. We toured about three years with Derrick at the helm. It was a rewarding time for Lagwagon. We had so much fun. Derrick and I used to buy instant coffee and right before a show we would stir a large tablespoon of it into a glass of Mountain Dew soda, then pound it. If you made it through the show without pooping your pants, you were golden.

The studio experience was something completely different. The studio was less forgiving. The details were a new priority. Attention to the tightness and tuning fought instinct and emotional performance. This was difficult for all of us, especially Derrick. By our third album the microscope was out. That album was *Hoss* and it would be Derrick's last with Lagwagon. We had an actual budget. It was our first effort working with producer Ryan Greene, who later would be associated with "The Fat Sound," a nod to Fat Wreck Chords' early catalogue. When we were writing and making demos for *Hoss*, it all started to fall apart. There were growing inner-band issues, deep resentments developed on tour that went largely ignored.

On top of all that, during the years of touring between our second album, *Trashed,* and *Hoss*, Derrick had picked up a drug habit. He made little effort to hide it, so by the time we were making the *Hoss* demos, the dope and quiet feuds were taking a toll on all of us. The issues were out in the open. It amazes me still how loaded Derrick was during the *Hoss* sessions and that he still managed to make an album that is seminal and iconic to many drummers. I have wondered since what it could have been. Flip stayed with him in the drum room and poured pots of coffee down his throat while I sat with Ryan, who had only just met us, in the control room. I am proud of the record, but it also marks the end of our era with Derrick. We were withering just as we had begun to blossom.

On the first tour following the release of *Hoss*, all the anxiety came to a head. No one spoke much on the drives, and Derrick flirted with overdosing every day. From California, we made it as far as The Nite Owl in Pensacola, Florida. That night, on stage, mid-set, all of the tension finally reached a breaking point. A yelling match between our two giant guitar players, Flip and Shawn Dewey, turned into a fist fight. It wasn't unlike the 1966 Japanese film *The War of the Gargantuas*. This was it, the fever pitch.

We exploded on stage in front of a packed house. The brawl made its way off stage into the green room and Derrick nodded out, falling through his kick drum off the drum riser to the middle of the stage. Our one crew hand, Bryan Radinski, was yelling obscenities and kicking Derrick. "This is all your fucking fault." I looked to our bass player, Jesse Buglione, for a shred of sanity. As he was lighting a cigarette, he tilted his head, pointed his eyes, and gestured toward the stunned and silent crowd. That was that. Tour over. Band over. Game over. We were done, or so I thought. Well, at least Derrick was done. I couldn't imagine Lagwagon without him at the time, but I learned to.

There were a few attempts to get Derrick sober, but, by his own assertion, he chose dope over the band. In hindsight, the band's hiatus seemed like forever. In reality, it was likely only six months later when Dave Raun joined us and we resumed touring for a year in support of *Hoss*. Some relationships improved while others worsened, but that's another story. This is about Derrick.

Lagwagon plowed on making records and touring as Derrick and I stayed in touch and our relationship continued. Many years passed. I moved to San Francisco, but frequently travelled south to visit Santa Barbara and occasionally Derrick. Eventually, I realized he'd kicked drugs and, at some point, we discussed making music together again. Shortly after, a music project began with a childhood friend Marko DeSantis [Sugarcult]. At first the three of us would simply get together, drink, and experiment with songs I had written that didn't suit Lagwagon. Marko may have been the only one that thought these good times would amount to anything more than fun. He was right. After a few poorly recorded demos at the rehearsal space, Bad Astronaut was born. The very first song was called "Catherine Morgan," a nod to our reprise, Derrick's friend Catherine and "Captain Morgan," the spiced rum we consumed by the bottle at rehearsals. The first lines in the song say it all: "It's strange to be here with D, among the strange but, it had to be, over the jams, over the ice, sheltered from the sun." Bad Astronaut went on to become a studio project with six group members, recording three full-length albums. It was and will always be my favorite musical endeavor shared with Derrick Plourde.

Speaking of Derrick's "legacy," I always cite more than his musical contributions. It's a legacy of words and behavior. I have never known anyone with his wit or character. He inspired so much more than the music in my life. He was the author of so many words and coined so many phrases (many of which are still in use or rotation, especially in song). So many of these are standards in other bands—"Punisher," "Team," "Matters," "Stoke Extinguisher," and "Bad Astronaut" to name a few. He would remain silent for days and then, in a sudden outburst, would shout something perfectly appropriate to whatever was happening. Derrick was brilliant, a master quipper, a natural poet. He was complex and you had to work to gain his respect. I appreciate that more than ever now.

In memory of Derrick Plourde (October 17, 1971—March 30, 2005).

Suggested Tracks

Lagwagon:
"Lazy" and "Stokin' the Neighbors" from *Trashed*
"Rifle" and "Move the Car" from *Hoss*

Bad Astronaut:
"Logan's Run" and "Greg's Estate/Anecdote" from *Acrophobe*
"Disarm" from *Houston: We Have A Drinking Problem*
"Ghostwrite" from *Twelve Small Steps, One Giant Disappointment*

Joey Cape *is the lead singer and songwriter for the iconic punk band Lagwagon. His other bands include Me First and the Gimme Gimmes, Bad Astronaut, Scorpios, The Playing Favorites, and Bad Loud. Joey also has a successful solo career including nine albums. He has toured worldwide extensively the past thirty years.*

TOP FIVE POP PUNK DRUMMERS

By Marko DeSantis

LIKE POWER POP, R&B, and punk itself, pop punk as a genre is a generational moving target that means many things to many people. Ask an older person and they'll probably assume you're describing something like the Ramones, the Buzzcocks, or more likely the Descendents, the Replacements, Hüsker Dü, and the Dead Milkmen. Ask that person's younger sister and they'd probably assume you meant Screeching Weasel, Green Day, NOFX, the Queers, even early/pre-Hot-AC era Goo Goo Dolls. Ask her less-cool younger cousin who grew up in the 'burbs and he might tell you about Jimmy Eat World, MXPX, the Ataris, Nerf Herder, and all the late nineties/early aughts bands that emerged from cul-de-sacs and shopping mall food courts to surf the tsunami-sized cultural wake of Blink-182's giant radio records; bands like New Found Glory, Good Charlotte, Sum 41, All Time Low, Simple Plan, Yellowcard, the Starting Line, and All American Rejects.

Maybe their brooding, black clothes-clad step-sibling who was conceived to the sound of Cure and Fugazi records would offer up their version of the truth and talk about the darker side of the same pop-punk coin reluctantly referred to as emo (or alternatively, "screamo" if it included a guttural vocalist and was weighted with a heavier metal edge); bands like Taking Back Sunday, Finch, My Chemical Romance, the Used, Paramore, Fall Out Boy, etc. Ask a kid today and they'd shrug and say, "IDK, prolly that new Machine Gun Kelly or those early 5 Seconds of Summer records from way back in 2014 that sound kinda like throwbacks to some old school shit like Hot Chelle Rae meets the Summer Set, LOL." (Note: These artists' debut records only came out in 2009; kids today!)

My band Sugarcult fell off our dive bar stools, cut our debut record, and as we aimlessly walked alone with no genre to call our own, somehow got taken in like rescue animals by the traveling circus of the 2001 Warped Tour and were welcomed with loving hoodie-sleeved arms into the group hug of the emerging early aughts pop-punk party. For better, or for worse…but it was a hell of a lot more fun than the previous iteration of our audience: jaded Los Angeles club goers, arms crossed, in cooler jackets, slowly sucking down overpriced Stellas, and enduring our set until their friends' band went on. The pop-punk craze offered us amnesty from probable obscurity, granted us immediate teenage rock and roll citizenship, and let us do as we pleased. Pop punk never dared ask us to learn their native tongue (mostly the language of dick jokes and pep rallies), alter our aesthetic, adopt their tropes, or god-forbid don their atrocious Hot Topic-sourced fatigues. We said "fuck it" and made ourselves at home.

It turned out to be a good deal as the clunky, awkward genre glowed up into a full-on youth movement that defined the cultural moment and set the tone for the early twenty-first century. We got to play in sports arenas touring the USA and Japan with Green Day on their *American Idiot* comeback, and with Blink-182 on their Europe/UK run. For almost ten years, we played enormous festivals and toured domestically and internationally with different configurations of most of the aforementioned bands (Good Charlotte, Ataris, MXPX, etc.). We became good friends with these bands as we got to know them as individuals. What's more, we eventually broke our inner-music-snob guards down and developed a deep appreciation for how good most of them were as songwriters and as musicians.

It was humbling when you watched these players up close, night after night. And, most importantly for this collection, these groups were loaded with some world class drummers. (Sugarcult was lucky to be powered by two fantastic drummers during our decade-long run, Kenny Livingston and Ben Davis before him, but it would be in bad taste to name your own band mates, now wouldn't it?)

Here are a few pop-punk drummers from our travels who we had big musical crushes on:

Tré Cool
Green Day

Green Day's resident Keith Moon was always a marvel. Night after night, he relentlessly plowed through the band's three-hour set. Flashy, fun, furious, and flawless. Tré always seemed to be up to some kind of hijinks: buying ice cream for a bunch of strangers to cheer them up as they waited in a hopeless line at the airport; keeping a fully stocked bar in a road case behind his kit, with a bartender at the ready should a band member fancy a mid-show refreshment; handing his sticks to random kids pulled from the audience and letting them play his kit. That kind of drummer.

Ilan Rubin
Denver Harbor, Angels & Airwaves

We first encountered this boy-wonder on Warped Tour 2002, when he was only fourteen years old and playing in the band

Denver Harbor. Word quickly got around on the tour about this kid who could play circles around pros twice his age. He would grow up to play in Angels & Airwaves with Tom DeLonge from Blink-182. Eventually Ilan landed on the drum throne of Nine Inch Nails, who were inducted into the Rock and Roll Hall of Fame in 2020, making Ilan (now barely thirty) the Hall's youngest living inductee. He's also a guitar virtuoso, the bastard!

Branden Steineckert
The Used

We met the Used in late 2001 when we played a tour date in Utah and they were added as local support; I remember putting a five-dollar bill in the tip jar they were passing around the venue, like some kinda punk rock tithing. A year later, they had been signed, and we shared a tour bus with them on Warped Tour 2002. The Used's debut record was an instant classic and single handedly changed the entire game; the way new bands sounded, played, and looked. Branden was straight edge, a total sweetheart, but dead serious about honing his craft. He went on to become the drummer of Rancid, who he had once confided to me was his all-time favorite band.

Tony Thaxton
Motion City Soundtrack

Motion City Soundtrack opened for us for our first Euro/UK headlining tour in 2003. It was an arranged marriage through our bands' mutual label, Epitaph Records, who put our record out overseas. Luckily, we hit it off and they quickly became one of our favorite bands in the scene. Like us, they were kinda genre outsiders who had been co-opted by the pop-punk/emo explosion under the guise of being heralded as the next Get Up Kids or something.

They were delightful Midwestern weirdos with impeccable record collections and vintage gear. Tony was an artisan of a drummer, perfectly framing their angular guitar parts and the manic genius of front man Justin Pierre.

Travis Barker
Blink-182

Like a front man trapped in a drummer's body, Travis is as iconic as he is charismatic. But despite the tattoos, reality shows, side-hustles, hip-hop ventures, and fame and fortune, he has a punk-rock soul and is at his core a *musician's* musician. With the possible exception of Lagwagon's Derrick Plourde, I've never seen a drummer more tirelessly dedicated to his instrument. You'll rarely find Travis without a pair of sticks in his grasp, tapping beats on practice pads, magazines, tatted thighs, or furniture whenever he's away from his kit. His nuanced, intricate technique combines with Blink's simple, catchy melodies and makes it sound like magic. They bring the pop, he brings the punk.

Marko DeSantis *is a music professional best known as the lead guitarist and cofounder of Sugarcult, with whom he toured worldwide and sold over a million records since launching out of Santa Barbara, California, in 2001. Marko has also written, recorded, and toured in bands such as Bad Astronaut, Popsicko, The Ataris, Swingin Utters, and Nerf Herder. As an educator, DeSantis holds professor residencies at several colleges and music business programs. He is based in Los Angeles.*

TRÉ COOL OF GREEN DAY

Interviewed by S. W. Lauden

T RÉ COOL WAS STILL a tween when he embarked on a crash course in punk drumming by studying bands like Bad Brains, 7 Seconds, and X, and later watching drummers from bands like Operation Ivy, MDC, and Mr. T Experience. He joined Green Day in 1990, debuting on the East Bay band's second album, *Kerplunk!* Over the course of a successful thirty year career, Tré Cool has established himself as a pop-punk icon who remains true to his roots while continually challenging himself to improve and evolve. I caught up with him by phone while Green Day was on The Hella Mega Tour with Fall Out Boy, Weezer and the Interrupters.

When did you start playing drums?

I was eleven. I went over to Lawrence Livermore's place [musician/cofounder of Lookout Records] because my friend was playing with him [in the Lookouts]. He had a drummer, but it was his girlfriend and she left him to move to Brazil. He kept the drum set, so kind of by default I said, "I'll play." I didn't know what I was doing, but I went into the jam space there with Larry and Kain Kong. They already had a bunch of songs like "My Mom Smokes Pot," "I Want To Love You, But You Make Me Sick," "Fuck Religion"—stuff like that. I just started bashing away, hitting the cymbals and thinking "this is fun." So, Larry stops and says "Let's take your cymbals away. Learn to play the drums first and we'll start giving you cymbals when it's time."

So I concentrated on learning beats, but it was really fast music. Larry gave me these tapes and told me to listen. The tapes had bands like 7 Seconds, MDC, Dead Kennedys, X, Bad Brains—stuff like that. He said, "Listen to this shit and try to sound like that."

Wow. Tall order.

7 Seconds was the closest to what we were doing at the time. I thought, "Basically it's like Polka on methamphetamines." I just started earning my cymbals, like badges of honor.

We played our first show and everybody ran away. We played another show and got unplugged. I think we were doing it right.

What was the first drum set that you owned?

That drum set I was playing on technically was Larry's at the time. It was a sixties Ludwig Ringo [Starr] kit with the Black Oyster Pearl finish. I used to have to nail it to the floor because it would slide away. Then as a sort of Christmas/birthday present, when I turned thirteen my dad picked up a Pearl Export kit. It was a six-piece, so it was massive for a little kid. It was a fiberglass kit with red shells. That's what I recorded *Kerplunk* on. I still have most of that kit.

Chris Appelgren was using that original Ludwig kit in the Potatomen. It was Larry's kit, but I think he sold it. It was covered in stickers and had been thrown off of stages and into the backs of vans. Many years later, Chris gave me a call and said he had something for me, and it was *that* kit. He had cleaned it up, taken the stickers off and gotten the goop off. He said, "I think you should have this since it's the first kit you ever played." That was pretty bad ass. So, now I have that kit again, in its entirety.

Amazing. What a great gift.

That was a really cool thing to do. Chris also ran Lookout Records for a long time after Larry left.

Then, when we were going to make *Dookie*, we got some money to buy new equipment. So I went and bought a DW kit with the same finish as that original Ludwig kit, and a Noble and Cooley snare—which was the holy grail. I've played that snare on every Green Day record since. Maybe not the entire record, but there's at least one song on every record with that *Dookie* snare. I toured it, it got Woodstock '99 mud all over it. I bring it to every session.

Then I got a DW endorsement. I ordered a giant red sparkle kit with every size tom, from 8" all the way down to 20". A couple different-sized kick drums and snares. Then I started knocking them over and the DW guys were like 'Hey. You can't smash our artisanal drums like that. That's not what our company's about. We'll kick you off.' You know? So then I made a video where we threw the drums off a cliff and ran them over with a bulldozer in a garbage dump.

So, I left DW and played Ayotte drums for a hot second, and then Slingerland. Slingerland was fine with me lighting them on fire, kicking them down stairs, throwing them into the Bay—whatever. I burned entire semi truckloads of Slingerland drums. They sort of went out of business—I wonder why? [Laughs]

Then I got a Ludwig endorsement, and they were great, but I started collecting antique drums and stuff. I was into Leedy because my favorite snare was a thirties Leedy. I started researching Leedy to see who owned them because I wanted to buy the company and revamp it—bring it back to its former glory, but manufacture the drums in Oakland or somewhere like that. I found out that Fred Gretsch owns Leedy and bought it primarily for some of the patents they had. I talked to him and he said 'Let's revamp it.' So, they made me a bunch of kits and we went to NAMM [the National Association of Music Merchants' annual trade show] and stuff, but they were expensive, so it didn't really take off. I went to Gretsch from there. They were a great company and really took good care of me.

Then I discovered SJC and really liked what they were doing. There's a lot of attention to detail and if I have crazy ideas, they'll work with me. That shit sounds insane, so I respectfully left Gretsch on good terms and switched to SJC. Those are the drums I'm playing now.

You've played all the great American drum kits, but you left out Pork Pie.

Bill [Detamore] made me a kit, but it didn't really work out for what I was trying to do at the time—which was destroy. I felt bad because I thought, "These are too nice. I don't want to smash these around."

You mentioned bands like 7 Seconds, MDC, and Bad Brains earlier. Who were some of your drum heroes when you first started playing?

It was basically people I'd play gigs with. Dave Mello [Operation Ivy], Alex Laipeneiks from Mr. T Experience, Al [Schvitz] from MDC—guys I'd play shows with. I'd play my gig and then just watch them. A lot of times I'd just sit on a milk crate behind them and watch them do their thing. I mean, playing with NoMeansNo at Own's Pizza was life changing; watching [John Wright] just rip.

He was probably the best punk drummer ever. I was standing right behind him and couldn't help but suck that stuff up as a twelve or thirteen-year-old kid. I knew exactly what I wanted to do in life. There was never any "Cover your bases. Learn a trade." Fuck that. Just play drums. I didn't even graduate high school. I was like, "I'm not playing drums enough right now because I'm wasting time at school."

When I listen to your drumming, I also hear the influence of British Invasion drummers like Ringo Starr and Keith Moon. Did any of that music resonate with you?

Yeah. That's what I was listening to, but I never really got into playing along with albums on headphones. I tried when I first started drumming, when I was trying to get the independence with my right foot and my left hand, learning to play polyrhythms and that kind of stuff. I would play along to the Cars. Those songs have nice, solid beats that are really steady, but that's where it kind of stopped. I was off to the races and just blazed.

But, listening to records is something I always liked to do. The stuff Ringo was doing, while overlooked by a lot of kids my age—or even scoffed at—meant a lot to me because he was doing just the right thing. He's hitting the dynamics just perfect, he's playing to the song, there are hooks there. That's an important part of drumming, learning to hear the hooks instead of just bashing the beat.

With Keith Moon, it was just the balls out energy, the craziness of it, which appealed to me. He just checked all the boxes for me as a real hero. And AC/DC for learning pocket. Those are the elements you need to be a really good drummer— you need pocket, you have to be able to be a little unhinged, you need hooks, and you've got to play to the song.

Are there any modern drummers you like to listen to?

Jesse Bivona from the Interrupters is incredible. Obviously, Josh Freese is fun to watch because he can fucking do everything... you son of a bitch! [Laughs] And the band Black Pumas—they're not punk rock, but that drummer [Stephen Bidwell] has his shit together.

You've been playing with Green Day for thirty years now. How do you think your drumming has evolved in that time?

I don't speed up as much as I used to. Tempo is something I constantly have to address and struggle with. On [The Hella Mega Tour], I start a lot of songs, and I'm coming out of another song with a different tempo and different feel. The whole band's counting on me to get that first measure right, so I have to nail those tempos.

And I think physical endurance is important too. I'm forty-eight-years-old now, and I'm playing the same shit that I made up when I was nineteen. You just keep working on it.

If I was going to climb on the Green Day bus tonight, what music would I hear?

Probably a really loud ringing in your ears... [Laughs]

Maybe I'd start off with a little Bill Withers. Move on to some Black Sabbath. Then, gently slide into, I don't know, Blowfly. And finish it off with Tom Waits or something.

If you met a young drummer who was looking to start a punk band today, what advice would you give them?

I would say—to keep it short—protect your hearing. Always use earplugs. Or, if you can get your band on in-ear [monitors], get in-ears. Very, very important.

Otherwise, don't fuck anybody over. The little things add up and fuck up the big things. And, on the flip-flop, the little things could add up to create great things.

DARE YA TO DO WHAT YOU WANT

By Mindy Abovitz

G INA WAS AT THE drum kit in her miniskirt, intermittently
flashing us, and hitting harder than any dude I had ever seen.
My living room was filled with her punky beats, and I knew that
I would never be the same for it. Her rhythms and unapologetic
playing reawakened the obsession I had with Riot grrrl when
I was a teenager and Bikini Kill and Slant 6 songs lived rent-free in
my head. But this was the early 2000s, the next wave of feminism,
amplified. I had been waiting a decade for this.

Don't You Talk Out of Line

I grew up in Hollywood, Florida. When I was one, my parents
rented out a two-bedroom for the five of us and we spent our
weekends flinging ourselves into the ocean and building sand
burgers. We were a big, loud, and loving family: cousins, aunts,
uncles, and the two pillars of the tribe, our grandparents. Our
neighborhood block was lined with palm trees and the median
age of our neighbors was seventy-five.

My parents and their parents grew up in Israel/Palestine,
and when they moved to the US, they brought their culture and
religion with them. I grew up singing Hebrew songs and banging
on the table each weekend, as we sat down for Shabbat and

holiday meals. Everyone sang off-key with the confidence of an Italian opera singer. The "band" included my dad striking plates and cups with utensils, my Saba (grandfather) bringing in sweet melodies, Shamai (his best friend) harmonizing, and the rest of us meeting their cacophony with our own. This type of music-making—free, unapologetic, and open for interpretation—runs in my blood.

My parents' only option for exposing us to Judaism in the United States was to send us to a Modern Orthodox Jewish day school. There I learned Hebrew, Talmud, Chumash, and that girls and boys have different roles in life. I was left to sit out many of the honors my brothers and male cousins took part in like reading from the Torah and having a significant rite of passage to adulthood. They also prayed in the men's section of the synagogue, close to all the action, while I was relegated to the women's section, yards away and behind a wooden partition. An early indication that I was beginning to feel like an outsider in this religious atmosphere was my choice to dress up as an alien at my own Bat-Mitzvah (a party to celebrate religious maturity and coming of age). There I was, trading in the traditional frilly pink dress and push-up bra for silver face paint, green lips, and thigh-high metallic boots, a foreshadowing of what was to come.

You're a Big Girl Now

In the mid-nineties, I was a tenth grader at a public high school that was not religious and not challenging. It left my new best friends and I loads of free time to attempt ollie after nose stall after kick-flip after ollie on our skateboards, and to deep fangirl any punk band that dared drive that far south. When those handful of bands arrived, they had a choice of two venues to play in Miami: Cheers or Churchill's Pub. Attending those shows as a teen meant jumping into the car with anyone who had one. That was often the coolest girl in my school, Lisa Bromley. It was on one of those car rides that she passed me Bikini Kill on cassette and told me to press play.

Up until that moment, music was polished; recorded well by folks who knew their way around their instrument. I loved music, but it felt far away from me. Kathleen Hanna scream/singing about what mattered to her (which subsequently mattered to me) while sloppy instrumentation held up her pissed-off voice was an invitation for me to get involved. "Double Dare Ya" had my name on it. Sporting a shaved head with multi-colored spikes and a dog collar around my neck, I hung my head out the window of Lisa's 1960s Valiant and wailed every lyric to *Revolution Girl Style Now!* from her beat-up back seat.

The pivotal elements to Bikini Kill's ultimate influence on my musical upbringing were the members of the band, particularly Tobi Vail. Tobi was the first female drummer to make an imprint on my brain. Drums are loud, angry things that you have to hit in order to make them sing. Your legs are spread open when you play, and your arms go flailing about. Muscles help you hit them harder, and stamina keeps you going longer. The likelihood of your getting sweaty at the kit is pretty high, but Tobi didn't seem to care. She was a girl, banging things and unafraid to sweat on a stage. She took up lots of space and was loud. Tobi's drumming went against everything I was taught and I loved it.

Dare Ya to Do What You Want

I moved to Gainesville, Florida, mostly by accident. I hadn't put much thought into where I would go to college, but University of Florida offered me a free ride so that's where I landed. Lucky for me, the town was crawling with musicians, vegans, and bike-punks, and North Florida wasn't too far off the map for touring bands. I found a home amongst tatted-up line cooks who couldn't wait to get off work to jam with their mates. They would plug in their instruments and mics and sit at their kits and I would watch. On a tattered sofa of one of the many punk houses where I hung out, I was fangirling again. Then I realized: I didn't know any girls who were making music in our scene. It reminded me of my Orthodox upbringing and of being sat in the women's section, which was far from the stage. I left that world because I needed to get my hands dirty, only to end up on a couch—an arms-reach from the action—as a spectator again.

What would Tobi do?

That was my wake-up call. I'd impatiently wait until my friends set off for work, then promptly sit at their drum sets. I was loud, awful at drumming, and the happiest I had been in a long time. Arms flailing about and as free to express myself as I had learned to be at my family's Shabbat dinner tables. I was finally on my path. At the time, I was booking shows at the local zine library/ info shop, the Civic Media Center, where I befriended (and often booked) the new band, Against Me! Lil' Kev (as Kevin Mahon was known at the time) was drumming with Laura Jane Grace—it was just the two of them—and he became my first informal drum instructor. He taught me rudiments and basic beats on buckets and those were some of the best lessons I got.

You've Got No Reason Not to Fight

Choosing to move to New York City in the early 2000s was not difficult. I was now fully obsessed with music, had been in two bands, and was ready to be a small drummer fish in a big musical pond. New York was a grind (no duh, right?). My Riot grrrl-self thought that I would meet other ladies to make sweet music with in no time, but instead I spent my first few years there looking hopelessly for my dream bandmates. In the meantime, I started a one-person band called More Teeth, which involved me, a Madonna mic, my drum kit, a Dr. Rhythm drum machine, and a Dr. Sample sampler strapped to my bass drum. I practiced in a shithole of a space (literally a cave I could not stand up in) and performed anywhere anyone would have me.

I thought More Teeth would lead me to my future musical family and it did! A short two years later, Jee Young Sim spotted me playing in my solo act opening up for legit bands in my punk house The Woodser. Jee later became my longest-running bandmate ever. Everyone I lived with was in one or two bands at the time (the Good Good, Mahogany, Brasilia) and we set our house up as one-half living space and one-half show space. We put shows on in our house nearly every weekend from 2003–2008. We bought shit liquor, set up a makeshift bar, took some money at the door, and ran the sound. We typically kept the bar money for the house and gave the bands the door. TV on the Radio, Matt & Kim, Amps for Christ, White Magic plus hundreds of bands you've likely never heard of (Grass Widow, Kickball, Defiance, Ohio, Callers, Bonedust, Holopaw) played in my living room.

Cue Gina Marie Scardino, the drummer from the opening of my story. Gina was in a local Brooklyn punk trio called Breaker! Breaker! Gina was the drummer who hit hardest, played in a frayed miniskirt, and couldn't give a fuck. She was everything I dreamt of when I set out to meet the baddest musicians in NYC.

And it was a photo of her I used on the first-ever flier announcing *Tom Tom Magazine's* existence.

I Got a Proposition, Goes Something Like This

In 2009, Riot grrrl was making a resurgence, bringing a new wave of punk feminism to girls just as it had when I was in my teens. But something about this revival felt unsettling to me. The revolution we had hoped for back in the nineties had not materialized. The kinds of women I saw beating seven shades of hell out of drum kits in clubs and basements around the country had not made it to the covers of the magazines on music shop shelves. When you typed "girl drummer" into Google Images, you'd see a cascade of scantily clad models draped over drum kits and articles titled, "Can Girls Really Play the Drums?"

I decided that if these powerful, mesmerizing women I knew weren't going to be represented by the old media, then I had to become the media. If we couldn't get a seat at the kit, we needed to kick over the cymbals and make some noise. The fusty, closed world of traditional representation was the problem, and *Tom Tom Magazine* was going to be the solution.

In that first image, Gina is standing in her bike shop (King Kog) holding her snare and staring down the camera lens. The photo embodied everything *Tom Tom* was going to be: an independent woman, standing in the shop she owns, holding a piece of her kit, and confidently challenging you or anyone to try and take it away from her. The back of the flier read:

> *T O M T O M M A G A Z I N E* is the portal for information about females that drum. *Tom Tom's* purpose is to raise awareness about girl and women drummers from all over the world and to inspire females of all ages to drum. *Tom Tom's* goal is to strengthen and build the community of otherwise fragmented female musicians and to create a network of musicians around the world. *Tom Tom* serves a unique purpose by catering exclusively

to female drummers and providing them with important information and resources. Based out of the most exciting city in the world...Brooklyn, NY.

The first two print issues of *Tom Tom* featured drummers I knew, wanted to know, and was about to know. Frankie Rose (Frankie Rose + the Outs), Kim Schifino (Matt & Kim), Stella Corkery (White Saucer), Ali Koehler (Vivian Girls), LaFrae Sci (Burnt Sugar), JD Samson (Le Tigre), Shannon Funchess (Light Asylum), and Hannah Blilie (the Gossip) filled those introductory pages. By issue three, we were featuring globally recognized drummer's drummers like Cindy Blackman Santana (Santana, Lenny Kravitz) on the cover. Once we got started, responsibilities grew and I understood what a large undertaking this was going to be.

Running the only print magazine in the world focused on female/gender non-conforming (GNC) drummers, beatmakers, and producers has been equal parts rewarding, exhilarating, impossible, and exhausting. It became quickly obvious that not only was it wildly important to create a home for all of us female drummers, but that there was massive under-representation for drummers of different ages, races, ethnicities, ability levels, sexualities, gender identities, body sizes, religious beliefs, and skill levels. Being the best drummer has never been important to me. Being an inspiring drummer always has. That and equal representation have been the governing compass of our magazine from day one.

I have spent the last ten years of my life revering female/GNC drummers, beat makers, and producers in print, online, and real life. I am inspired daily by the millions of Ginas I have uncovered through running *Tom Tom*. Drumming got me here, and I am finally home.

Mindy Abovitz *is an award-winning entrepreneur and social activist, committed to diversifying the music industry. She is the publisher and CEO of* Tom Tom Magazine *and cofounded Hit Like a Girl. Mindy inspires a global audience of musicians to play with power, pride and to be seen. She was recognized by the Grammys as a Change Agent and is the recipient of the She Rocks Award.*

STEVEN MCDONALD OF REDD KROSS

Interviewed by S. W. Lauden

R EDD KROSS BASSIST, STEVEN McDonald, is a lifer. He discovered punk rock in 1977 at the age of ten. The band he formed with his older brother recorded their debut six-song EP, *Red Cross*, when Steven was only twelve. Their first full-length album, *Born Innocent*, came out in 1982; the band's most recent album, *Beyond the Door*, was released in 2019. In between, Redd Kross has toured and recorded with a revolving throne of drummers ranging from Ron Reyes, John Stielow, and Janet Housden to Victor Indrizzo, Brian Reitzell, and Roy McDonald. In recent years, Steven has also played with drummers Mario Rubalcaba in the band OFF!, and Dale Crover in Melvins and Redd Kross.

You're a bass player who has been recording and touring around the punk universe since the late seventies. In your opinion, what makes for a great punk drummer?

Energy and the ability to keep the energy up. It's not about Neil Peart precision, at least for me. To me, early Ringo Starr was a really great example of that kind of raw expression—the splashy, trashy, joyful pounding that my favorite punk drummers did in the late seventies.

That's interesting. I think a lot of people would point to Keith Moon as the British Invasion inspiration for punk drumming.

Keith Moon definitely had a sort of unorthodox, fuck-you approach, but it was so ornamental that it ultimately has more in common with other forms of music that punk was trying to strip down when it started. I love all of his flashy fills and they're done in a punk spirit...but he was definitely more of a shock rocker.

Outside of your own bands, who are some punk drummers that you admire?

The Ramones were the band that changed my way of thinking about music. I always have to give the credit to my brother, Jeff, who is three-and-a-half years older than me. He already had the sophisticated musical tastes of somebody five to ten years older than him. So, usually my interviews read like I'm in my midsixties, but when I talk about hearing the Ramones in 1977, I was only ten years old at the time.

I just found a YouTube video of a Led Zeppelin concert that I attended when I was ten. It was June 23, 1977, at the Forum in Inglewood, California. And on the Keith Moon tip, he came out and played the timpani along with John Bonham during "Moby Dick" and just goofed around on stage. My experience is so weird because it's very rare that anybody my age actually saw Led Zeppelin. But in the time that lapsed between when we bought those tickets and when we went to the show, we discovered the Ramones—so we had already moved on in our tastes. The punk movement had changed the way I listened to music, and it changed my enthusiasm for being a part of music on some level. It was the first time my brother and I felt like we didn't just admire those musicians, we wanted to take a stab at being those musicians.

What was it about punk rock that inspired you?

To us it felt like this wasn't music made by wizards in some musical land that we'd never have access to. It felt accessible to little kids who were obsessives about music. Listening to Tommy Ramone play drums on those first three Ramones records, he just cut all the fat off and held down this backbeat that went back to early Beatles. That was music we were too young to have experienced the first time, so it spoke to us immediately. And then Marky Ramone after him when they put out *Road to Ruin* in 1978.

And I saw the Go-Go's a bunch of times in their early punk stages with the original drummer, Elissa [Bello]. She came up with great parts, but she didn't really glue the band together. I mean, I was twelve, so what did I know? I liked them okay, but they weren't my number one favorite band at the time. But then I saw their first show with Gina Schock, and she's a fucking great drummer; very consistent, super metronomic and plays dynamic fills. And the band went from one of my favorite bands on the scrappy punk scene to contenders on the world stage overnight. I got to witness that when I was a kid, and I realized that her drumming made a huge difference.

What about British punk bands?

The Damned were one of the bands that blew my mind. And their drummer, Rat Scabies, might be one of the reasons that people point to Keith Moon. He didn't have the same chops as a Keith Moon, but he had the same abandon. And obviously, Paul Cook on the first Sex Pistols record, which is just great meat-and-potatoes pub rock punk.

*Redd Kross has been around for over forty years, and in that
time you've toured and recorded with a variety of different
drummers. Was the revolving drum throne by design?*

It was all according to plan!

No, I think it's more a sign of the dysfunction and the wreckage.
My brother and I weren't always the most prolific songwriters
or the best leaders. We often tried to pawn responsibility off
on each other like fighting teenagers because we were fighting
teenagers. I'm sure it was tedious and didn't always inspire the
most confidence in our bandmates until we got into our twenties
and got more responsible.

*Were you finding the right drummer for the different
phases of the band? Or did the drummer help shape those
new directions?*

Probably a bit of both. I would say there are three things that help
bands go from scrappy to suddenly becoming quite presentable—
good songwriting, tuned guitars, and a great drummer…. As Jeff
and I progressed as musicians, I realized that when we had our
own "Gina Schock" behind us not only did the band suddenly
sound better, but I felt like a better bass player. It really upped our
game. The band is only as good as the weakest link.

*Roy McDonald played on two of my favorite Redd Kross
albums (Neurotica in 1987 and Researching the Blues in
2012), so I always think of him as the Redd Kross drummer.*

Roy's great. I've always been a big fan of his. Roy was thought of
as the Keith Moon of the scene that he came out of—and the band
we poached him from—because he was really flashy and had all
these great tom fills. That was also at the same time that our band
started getting really serious; I was finally out of high school,

Jeff was in his early twenties, we had a permanent rehearsal space and chances to tour. We'd probably stopped smoking weed, too. So, you can probably also hear all of that on *Neurotica* as well.

What was it like recording with Roy again for Researching the Blues *twenty-five years later*?

That record sounds like a real band album that was just bashed out in two weeks—and I wish that's the story I could tell—but it wasn't. We did rehearse that record in advance in a classic garage band style. Jeff had all these songs written, even if the lyrics weren't done, but we had a pretty good idea of what the melodies were. So, we bashed out those basic tracks in a week's time…and then the singing and mixing took another five years! I eventually ended up mixing that record myself, but it took me a long time to get the confidence to do it.

That record has an immediacy, it has an energy. It definitely sounds like a band record and I think that Roy is a big part of that. Playing with [guitarist] Robert Hecker and Roy did feel like home, that's for sure.

You've also played with drummer Mario Rubalcaba in OFF! What's it like playing hardcore punk at this point in your career?

The blueprint for OFF! is that first Black Flag line up and that's when I first started playing shows. My very first show was an eighth-grade graduation party, Redd Kross and Black Flag. Well, we were called the Tourists at the time, but we played an eighth-grade graduation party in Hawthorne, California, and we got Black Flag the gig before anybody knew who they were. So, I very much know in my bones what that genre is about; what Greg Ginn and Robo were inventing, and that's the spirit of what

OFF! was all about. Although Redd Kross never played music like that, we were more inspired by sixties beach movies and stuff.

But Mario's incredible. Of all the drummers I've played with, he has a John Bonham flavor. You talk about drum fills and feel, and how the drummer lands on the one after the fill—he was really good at holding back on it, while playing at break-neck paces. I learned a lot from playing with him.

More recently you and Dale Crover have been the rhythm section in both Redd Kross and Melvins. Any benefits to that kind of consistency for you across the two bands?

Dale's amazing. He also did a stint with OFF! when Mario went on hiatus to work on his band Earthless. That was really the entrance point for me playing with Dale in other projects. I'd known Dale and Buzz [Osborne, from Melvins] for years, but we hadn't been in contact for a while.

Dale is such a great guy and he's a great drummer. He's such a fan of music and that really comes through in his playing. The thing about Buzz and Dale is that they don't have a lot of the hang ups that other musicians have. They resolved themselves very early on that Melvins was their life. So, I would say that, by the late eighties, those two guys were just like, "This is it. This is just what we're doing. There is no plan b or plan c." They're committed to each other on some level and the band, which is probably why they can never hold onto a bass player. That's their particular sickness, and Redd Kross can never hold onto a drummer.

MY SELF-EDUCATION IN PUNK DRUMMING

By Kye Smith

I ALWAYS HAD AN interest in drumming. I remember seeing a video on *Australia's Funniest Home Videos* of a baby playing drums, and I thought it looked really cool. Something drew me to the whole setup of it.

I was twelve years old and attending my first music class in high school when I sat behind a drum set for the first time. It was around the same time that I began taking an interest in a different style of music. Green Day's music video for "Minority" was being played on Rage (which I guess is Australia's equivalent of MTV) and the whole cartoonish aesthetics of the clip coupled with the catchy melody of the music really piqued my interest. I took drum lessons for about six months before I got a drum kit of my own. I learned rudiments and sheet music—loving every chance I got to sit behind a kit—but I was more interested in figuring out how to play Green Day songs than music theory. Once I got a kit of my own for Christmas that year, I stopped lessons and spent every possible moment at home behind the kit. I never had a set of headphones loud enough to hear the music over the drums, so I would just play along to the songs in my head. I often completely forgot the structure of the song, but that didn't matter at the time—it was all about figuring how to play the fast rolls and seemingly impossible punk beat of bands like NOFX, Frenzal Rhomb, Lagwagon, and Blink-182.

This list, in no particular order, is an overview of songs I have found interesting, challenging, or especially fun to play over the years. I think a pitfall that a lot of young players fall into (including myself) is that technical parts seem better than simple parts and that the best drummers are the ones pulling out the wild fills. In reality, sometimes the most seemingly simple beats are the most effective, and while technicality has its place, it should not always be the end goal of a young player.

Everyone has their own interpretation of what "punk" means. As an Australian who grew up many years after the various waves of punk occurred, "punk" is an umbrella term that describes the broad style of rock music I was drawn to. Many punk elitists may argue that some of the bands on this list are not punk based on their own definition of the term, and that's fine. I'm not here to argue what is and isn't punk, whether it be a style of music or a lifestyle choice. Genre is not of high importance to me, it just so happens that many of the fast, melodic bands I grew up playing along to are often categorized under the punk banner.

"Welcome to Paradise"
Green Day—Dookie

Tré Cool has his own style and is the drummer that helped me understand the most about drumming while I was in the early stages of learning. Specifically, his kick drum patterns line up so well with the rhythm of Billie Joe Armstrong's guitar strumming that it allowed me to get a feel for how all the instruments intertwine rhythmically.

The part in this song I found most interesting was during the bridge build up. The first measure is bass driven, but over the course of the next few measures more guitar parts come in with Tré gradually adding to the drumbeat. He starts on the floor tom before adding kick, snare, and hi-hat. It is the last measure of this bridge that I always had a lot of trouble understanding, the incorporation of the ride bell always confused me. It sounded like you would need an extra limb to achieve these bells while still playing all the other parts. This was in the time before YouTube, so I didn't have the ability to watch a lot of live videos to see what was going on. While it's a bit of a juggle to make it work, it felt like a bit of an achievement when I finally figured it out. I think this song really speaks to Tré's drumming overall and is still one of my favorite drum parts.

"Greyhound"
Frenzal Rhomb—Sans Souci

Sans Souci is full of some of my favorite drum parts. This album was a huge catalyst in developing how I think about writing fills and interesting parts for songs rather than following the path of least resistance.

I remember listening to this song on my discman and feeling bewildered that Gordy Forman could play such fast rolls, especially during the chorus. In 2015, Gordy unfortunately broke his arm, and I was lucky enough to live the dream and fill in for him while his arm healed. This song was not a regular song on the setlist, but when asked what Frenzal songs I thought would be fun to add to the set I suggested this one. I immediately regretted it when I went to learn it since I had forgotten how fast those rolls were. We sound checked it one night, but never actually played it in front of an audience. I guess it wasn't tight enough to make the cut!

"Night Letters"
Propagandhi—Supporting Caste

This track was especially difficult for me because it is so far out of my NOFX-style comfort zone. Jord Samolesky is influenced by more metal and thrash than what I've spent time listening to, so the blast beats in this song were not something that I had the muscle memory for. I recorded a drum cover of this song in around 2012, and it was a fun challenge to figure out how to get through it (even if I didn't completely learn it hit for hit). After almost twenty years of drumming, I rarely need to count in my head while playing drums these days because the 4/4 style becomes intuitive after a while, but the different time signatures in this track meant breaking down each part and counting beats in my head. I also needed to add some extra toms and cymbals to my usual four-piece setup to play this song, which was a learning experience in itself.

"Rifle"
Lagwagon—Hoss

The forty-second drum intro to this song always stood out to me, even in the early years of learning to play. Derrick Plourde's style was so fluid and fast that I was entranced with this beat. Similar to a lot of other songs on this list, it seemed impossible to learn this song, but I challenged myself when I started recording drum covers for YouTube in 2012. Plourde moves around the kit so quickly that I had to change my set up slightly to make it work. I lowered the ride cymbal so it was right on top of the floor tom and tried to get the two toms and snare closer together. This song always really stood out compared to a lot of other drum parts in punk drumming at the time.

"Warning"
Green Day—Warning

With Green Day being my gateway band into punk rock and one of my biggest influences, I had to include two Green Day songs on this list. As I mentioned, *Warning* had just been released when I simultaneously started drumming and the title track was a fantastic place to start for a new drummer who had no ability to play some of the more complicated beats. This track has a slower pace compared to some other Green Day songs and it was also a great starting point to be able to listen to drums in a song and understand what is going on. The drums are clear in this mix, so it's easy to hear the bass drum pattern and open hi-hat in the verse. It's a really good song for someone in the early stages of learning to play this style of music.

"First Date"
Blink-182—Take Off Your Pants and Jacket

The sound of Travis Barker's drums on this album are so great. The super-tight snare is something that I strived to replicate for many years. This is probably one of the band's most covered songs by drummers on YouTube, thanks to really memorable drumming like the intro roll and the "let's go, don't wait" part. The bridge beat is really tricky as the bass drum follows the guitar strumming pattern while the hi-hat/snare pattern has a rhythm of its own. It's a level of coordination that still doesn't come naturally for me even after all these years of trying to play it.

"Injection"
Rise Against—The Sufferer & the Witness

This is my go-to, hard-hitting song. It has a nice mid-tempo so you can really let loose and get some aggression out. It's a really fun tempo to ride on the cymbals, and the fills that Brandon Barnes plays fit the song perfectly.

"The Decline"
NOFX—The Decline

This song is all about endurance. Playing the fast punk beat at the speed that Smelly (a.k.a. Erik Sandin) plays it for eighteen minutes straight would be really physically draining, but thankfully this song has so many different parts that there are a few chances to catch your breath. This was another of those bucket list songs that I wanted to learn when I started recording drum covers. Thankfully, I was already such a NOFX fan and had listened to it for years, so it came together a lot easier than I expected. I guess having developed the muscle memory for the punk beat from drumming along to other NOFX songs, it was just a case of remembering when the changes occur and what rolls Smelly plays in each part. For someone who has not grown up on this style of drumming, it could be a really tough challenge, kind of like if I were to attempt an eighteen-minute metal song.

I've heard Smelly in interviews discussing the writing/ recording of this song and how they treated it as a number of short songs, which is pretty much how I learned it as well. There is a part during the trumpet section where there is a ride bell in a syncopated rhythm, which I ignored when recording the cover as I think it might have been an overdub, but if Smelly played it at the same time as the other beat that is beyond my ability anyway!

"No Cigar"
Millencolin—Pennybridge Pioneers

Like many others, this song came to my attention in primary school while playing *Tony Hawk's Pro Skater 2* on Playstation, several years before I had any idea what punk rock was. It's a really fun song to play and one that has a nice driving drumbeat. The half time is a tempo that I really enjoy playing as it's not so fast that you need to pace yourself and you can really hit hard and have fun with it. Fredrik Larzon plays some fast doubles on the bass drum during the chorus, which is a fun trick that I have incorporated into a lot of my playing over the years as well.

"You"
Bad Religion—No Control

I was also introduced to this song via *Tony Hawk's Pro Skater* years before I listened to punk rock. Pete Finestone had a really distinctive style that was consistent throughout the Bad Religion albums he played on. This particular beat was one I learned very early on when I was getting drum lessons (at a much slower pace). It was the first time I had played the bass drum on the off-beat and it became my favorite beat at the time. Once I realized that it was a fairly standard punk beat, I immediately tried to figure out how to play it up to speed.

<>

THAT'S MY PERSONAL LIST of songs, but every player has their own strengths and weaknesses. A drum part that I struggled to figure out may come very easily to someone else and vice-versa. Music is very subjective and there are so many variables to learning an instrument; it is not a linear path to being able to play a certain song. It's a fun journey and I am still trying to learn as much as I can and be more creative every time I sit behind a kit.

Kye Smith *is an Australian session drummer. He is the creator of the "5 Minute Drum Chronology Series" on YouTube and has toured in bands such as Local Resident Failure, Frenzal Rhomb and The Porkers.*

ON A MOUNTAIN, ON A MOUNTAIN

by Ian Winwood

B ROOKS WACKERMAN JOINED BAD Religion at a pivotal point in the band's enduring career. Taking a seat on the drum stool following the departure of Bobby Schayer in 2001, the twenty-four-year-old Los Angelino became the punk group's sixth drummer, and the fifth to appear on either an EP or a full-length album.

During this time, there was a lot going on.

Twenty years after forming in the San Fernando Valley, at the turn of the century the quintet's five-album deal with Atlantic Records had run its course. Harvesting mixed results—from the masterful *The Gray Race* to the career low of *No Substance*—their seven-year spell as a smaller fish in a bigger pond had led, ultimately, to reduced returns and a declining profile. At this point, things could have gone either way for the band.

A Hollywood ending awaited them. Bad Religion returned to Epitaph Records; the independent label owned by former guitarist Brett Gurewitz, who originally founded it to release the group's music. After long wanderings away from the range, Bad Religion had finally come "home." So too did Gurewitz, seven years after resigning from the band he originally formed with singer Greg Graffin, bassist Jay Bentley, and drummer Jay Ziskrout in 1980.

The year was 1994, the summer in which punk rock broke the American mainstream for the first time. Green Day's *Dookie* went stratospheric, as too did *Smash* by the Offspring. The latter album was released by Epitaph; copies were pressed with money Gurewitz had raised by remortgaging his home. Wounded that his own band had decided to move to a major label—where they attained their first and only gold album for *Stranger Than Fiction*—Gurewitz stepped away from the life of a professional musician. For his return in 2001, a deal was made: "Mr. Brett," one half of Bad Religion's songwriting team, would compose and record material, but would not tour. This arrangement worked just fine. As well as the reunification of band and label, the conjoining of Brett and Greg saw the return of the finest double act in punk rock since Joe Strummer and Mick Jones.

So, yeah, there was a lot going on. With this in mind, it is surely understandable that even the band's most attentive constituents didn't immediately notice—or, at least, speak about noticing—the landscape-changing dynamic brought to bear by the hands and feet of Brooks Wackerman. It can be heard throughout *The Process of Belief*, the sextet's wildly applauded return to consistency, from 2002. It's there on the express train that is "Supersonic." It's there in the playful but accomplished opening of "Sorrow," one of Gurewitz's classic tracks, in which this atheist group once more tackled the concept of God. It's there in "You Don't Belong," Mr. Brett's paean to the punk rock community, in which Bad Religion have for decades played a pivotal role.

Wackerman was just getting started. Two years later, in 2004, the band released *The Empire Strikes First*, an even better album with a much-improved title. Here, the pyrotechnic finesse of the man who would become their longest-serving drummer, truly soars. From the cruise-control tempo of "Los Angeles is Burning" to the patient "Boot Stamping on a Human Face Forever," from the metal-edged blur of "Sinister Rouge" to the dexterous second act of "Let Them Eat War"—on which a nuanced groove allows Sage Francis to rap with flow and verve—this the work of a world-class player. On the final third of "Beyond Electric Dreams" ("On a mountain, on a mountain"), for my English pounds the finest song to which the group has placed its name, Wackerman's technique, and his dexterity, is such that I have been known to listen to what is barely a minute's worth of music for more than an hour. It is a remarkable achievement. With punk-rock chops, finally the group had the skills required to realize some of the ideas to which they hinted on *Into the Unknown* back in 1983.

Bad Religion has never had a problem writing songs. From their earliest days ("World War III," "We're Only Gonna Die," "Voice of God Is Government") to a bejeweled reemergence ("Forbidden Beat," "No Control," "Walk Away"), and on to the point at which Atlantic Records requested their presence on its storied roster ("American Jesus," "Hooray For Me...," "The Handshake"), the group has managed to imbue the airborne energies of punk rock with music that would bear scrutiny if played on only a single acoustic instrument. Nothing to worry about there. But where the band has sometimes proved deficient—not always wildly so, but so—is in marrying these compositions with players that are more than merely competent.

But that was then, and this is now. Over the course of more than forty years, on two occasions Bad Religion have absorbed a new member of such talent that the unit is improved immediately by a distance of galaxies. The first was the addition of Brian Baker, in 1994, who, as heard on the feloniously underrated *The Gray Race*, released the following year, brought fluid and melodic guitar solos to middle-eights that in the past had been the sites of mediocre musicians hacking away for all they were worth, which wasn't much. From 1995 on, listeners were treated to quality instrumental breaks on songs like "Drunk Sincerity," "Cease," "Candidate," and "Kyoto Now!" Baker is the finest lead guitarist in punk rock and Bad Religion would be lost without him.

They're not lost without Brooks Wackerman. With no hard feelings, the drummer left the group in 2015 to join Avenged Sevenfold, the arena metal group with a punk rock background. Here, he was able to expand the progressive pyrotechnics heard on "Beyond Electric Dreams" onto the vast and weird canvas of the fifteen-minute "Exist." For the past six years, Jamie Miller has kept the beat for Bad Religion, but keen-eared constituents each have their favorite drummer from the band's decades of active service. Me, I don't just think that Brooks Wackerman is the best to have played with Brian Baker, Jay Bentley, Mike Dimkich, Greg Graffin, Brett Gurewitz, and Greg Hetson—I think he's the best in the history of punk rock.

Have a listen to "Robin Hood in Reverse," or the group's explosive and ebullient version of "O Come All Ye Faithful." Go on, give 'em a spin. Tell me I'm wrong.

Ian Winwood *is an English music journalist and author who writes for the* Telegraph *and* Kerrang! *His forthcoming book,* Bodies: Life & Death In Music, *will be published by Faber & Faber on April 21, 2022.*

PHANIE DIAZ OF FEA

Interviewed by S. W. Lauden

FEA IS A FIERCE all-female, San Antonio-based punk band formed by drummer Phanie Diaz and bassist Jenn Alva in 2015. Born from the ashes of indie rock band Girl in a Coma, Fea has recorded two albums including 2019's *No Novelties*, produced by punk legend Alice Bag and released by Joan Jett's Blackheart Records. Over several tours, Diaz has learned a lot from drummers in the bands that Girl in a Coma and Fea have toured with including the Go-Go's, Morrissey, Social Distortion, and Babes in Toyland.

Were drums your first instrument?

I believe my first kit was a CB700. I used to mess around with our old drummer's kit in like 1994 when I played in a local band called Lady Dick with Jenn [Alva]. It wasn't until we started Girl in a Coma that I took on drums. I didn't want to, I was going to play guitar, but we just couldn't find the right female drummer. Jenn told me, "You can keep a beat, you do it." I didn't feel confident but thought, "Fuck it." She traded a guitar we had with a worker of hers for the drum set. I didn't even know how to set it up right. I remember it was Thanksgiving and we wrote a song as Girl in a Coma that night. Must have been 2001 or so.

Who were some of your favorite drummers early on?

I've always been a fan of punk, ever since I was a teen. I love the Cramps, Babes in Toyland, Bikini Kill, and then later got into the Smiths. I've always loved punk drumming and Lori Barbero [Babes in Toyland] has always been an influence of mine—hitting hard, being an extension of the drum. I always try to go nuts while drumming.

How have your drumming influences evolved over time?

I never considered myself a professional, even though I was making a living at it. So, I learned from watching the drummers from every band we toured with. Style, tricks, equipment preference. I got to tour with Morrissey, Sia, the Go-Go's, Cyndi Lauper, and Social Distortion. The list goes on and I learned from everybody. I will always be evolving as a drummer. You can be happy, but never satisfied. I think I play perfectly for what I do and that's enough for me. Always room to learn though.

What other music are you listening to these days? Any other drummers you like?

I've always been a fan of Meg White [the White Stripes]. She's the perfect example of playing what makes sense for that sound. Not going too overboard, just what's right for the song. Stephanie Luke [Rusty Coathanger of the Coathangers] is also one of my faves, and Janet Weiss [Sleater-Kinney] is another amazing drummer.

You and Jenn Alva formed your first band as teens—later adding your younger sister, Nina. What was the inspiration to start Girl in a Coma?

I wanted to start a band the day I saw Babes in Toyland with Jenn. They were touring with White Zombie and Melvins. I was so inspired by their power and sound that I knew right when we left, I wanted a band badly. Nina had been watching us and one day just busted out these amazing vocals. Despite the eight-year gap in age, we had her in front. Jenn and I wanted a sort of Riot grrrl band, but Nina's song writing style took us in a more indie direction (Fea was more the direction we had in mind); however, we are always proud of the sound the three of us created with GIAC.

You've recorded several albums and done many tours. Is there a difference for you between playing drums live and recording?

I personally always love playing live. It's unpredictable, raw, and exciting. I live for that. The studio has its own beauty though, watching a song transform into what you have to transcribe live. I watched Nina grow in confidence making each album and becoming her own performer. Though our first album, *Both Before I'm Gone*, put us on the map, I've always loved *Trio BC*. We dove into every genre, and we were definitely in tune at that time. We loved each other and what was happening with the band.

You and Jenn Alva formed your current band, Fea, in 2015. What would you say are the stylistic differences between the two bands?

I love Girl in a Coma. That band challenged me stylistically and gave me confidence, but Fea is the band I've always wanted. It's fun, it's dirty. My bandmates are laid back. I get to just thrash with that band. I also get to write, not just on drums but whole songs. Though it started like that with Girl in a Coma, with the success of the band, everyone had specific roles. It was hard to get out of that bubble.

How do you think being a drummer has changed your approach to songwriting?

Now that I drum, I just want to be an extension of the instrument. Not just play it and keep a tempo, but create a feeling—I want the beat to make you cry, make you excited. I've also learned to put on a show even though I'm seated. I see the song as a whole and not just a melody.

Fea released a self-titled debut album in 2016. Who was involved in making that album?

We started the album with Lori Barbero for three songs and then worked with Alice Bag of the Bags, followed by Laura Jane Grace of Against Me! It was amazing and each one of them taught us different approaches to our tunes.

No Novelties came out in 2019. How was that experience different than making the first album?

On the second album we worked solely with Alice Bag. She's amazing. She's like our music mom and very inspiring. She definitely pushes us in ways that we need. I think she understands that sometimes you don't have to be this trained musician to understand music. It's a feeling in the soul, and you either get it or you don't. You can learn all you need to learn, but if you don't feel it…how do you expect others to?

A TRIP TO TOMMY'S HOUSE

By Benny Horowitz

I GUESS, IF I THINK back, I've always liked hitting stuff.

And when the two cool girls in fourth grade joined school band, there was a rush of young boys suddenly interested in signing up, myself included. I chose the drums. Why not? I immediately had a knack for it, something I wasn't accustomed to. It was one of the first things that seemed to come easy to me.

My mom, a recent divorcee with three kids, took on a second job as a manicurist. As with anything, she had a tendency to go all in, quickly becoming a nail master and making a number of close friends. One night, driving to or from somewhere I can't remember, we stopped by her colleague's house on the outskirts of Somerville, New Jersey. Just through the front door, smack in the living room was a gigantic drum kit. I'm talking full-on late-eighties cannon glory.

Turned out this woman lived with her boyfriend, Tommy, who was a local rock musician. He was cool and let me fuck around on his kit. My mom drove us over there, off and on, for a number of months after that. She would smoke skinny cigarettes and drink tea in the kitchen with her friend while Tommy showed me how to play rock and roll songs.

It was totally informal. He'd pop on a record, sit down, and play to it while I watched. Then I'd eagerly wait for him to get up, so I could sit down and try it myself. It ended fairly quickly—and I never knew what happened to that guy—but it laid the groundwork. Sitting down and learning songs I love is still how I practice to this day.

Shortly after, I annoyed my mom for my first drum kit. It was a black, five-piece standard set-up with hardware and cymbals made by a company called Century. We forgot to buy a stool, so I used kitchen chairs for the first few years. I was jamming in my basement, mostly to eighties hair metal and early nineties grunge. A cool older kid at school, John Mopper, saw me wearing a Nirvana T-shirt and said he'd heard I played drums. I actually hadn't played in months at the time, so I'll never know if I would have lost them forever if he hadn't approached me. Perhaps. I've seen the dusty relics of childhood disinterest in the form of unused drums all over the world. Fortunately, I tried out for his band, playing "Come as You Are" by Nirvana. My course changed immediately.

I'll always remember my first show as the turning point, I can now see clearly as an old man. That band ended up being called Dilemma, and we played in a townie basement hosted by the singer of a band called the Rejected. We had three songs—one original called "Operation Liberation" and two covers, "A Bomb" by SNFU and "Bro Hymn" by Pennywise. People dug it so much that they asked us to play again after the Nirvana cover band, Verse Chorus Verse, finally ended. We did and it was a blast, although I really had no idea what was going on in the moment. I went to the front porch for air afterward, and an older girl from school came up and talked to me for a minute. It was innocuous, she just said hello and told me that we did a good job. That was it, but something clicked. This had to be it for me. Up until that point, with school, sports, and friend groups, I'd never felt relevant or necessary. And now, finally, I saw a path for myself, and I fucking jumped in headfirst.

Skip through a decade of playing in various bands and touring. I mostly ignored education, relationships, or any kind of serious employment that could stand in the way of my ultimate goal. I was cranking along and my road was coming to a head. I hit a point in my mid-twenties—broke and truly getting concerned about my future—when some old friends connected me with Brian Fallon. He had a previous band and tour that didn't work out, so he was cleaning house. I jumped in and it kickstarted a beautiful artistic connection that paved the way for a good portion of my life in the Gaslight Anthem.

It's always hard for me to pinpoint the moment I knew it would all work out. We used to have a bet that if we ever sold 10,000 records, we'd get throat tattoos. Our naive idea about the music business was that if you got to that point, you'd never have to work a real job again. That was really the ultimate goal, to sustain a life by only playing music. So, the first time we got a good opening slot, I thought we made it. Same with the first time we got a singalong from a crowd or sold one hundred dollars in merch.

Leap forward to seeing Bruce Springsteen's butt on a Glastonbury stage, having a Corona with Eddie Vedder, or jamming a Led Zeppelin song with half of the Bouncing Souls. It all blew my mind, and I don't let myself go very long without recognizing how special it all is. When you can manage to appreciate moments as they come, they all feel wonderful.

It took a lot of growth and adjustment, as a person and a player, to make it through that ride with the Gaslight Anthem. With the bulk of my formal training coming from elementary school and Tommy, I wandered into the woods of click tracks, arrangements, producers, and pro studios. Even learning how to properly hold and move an egg shaker was a big deal. I was nervous, and didn't really feel like I belonged, but loved the music and the band so much that I'd do anything to keep it going. It took a lot of heads-down, pride-swallowing, hard work, same as anything that's tough to achieve.

These days—as a father with quite a few creaky bones and great pride for the back catalog—I play, as always, for love. I've always felt a certain romance sitting in a room with songwriters, and that's still true today with my band Mercy Union. There's no better feeling than being moved by a new song in the moment; just floating in the air, waiting for ears. I also get boundless levels of energy playing drums with Antarctigo Vespucci.

Session work allows me to focus on instrumentation and arrangements, tapping into a part of my brain that yearns to be active. I'm still looking for the chance to feel relevant and good, just like on that porch years ago after my first show. We're all just one missed trip to Tommy's house away from a totally different life.

Benny Horowitz *is the father of two children and drummer for Mercy Union, The Gaslight Anthem, and Antarctigo Vespucci. He cohosts the* Going Off Track *music podcast, and* The Tune-Up *podcast.*

TOP FIVE DRUMMING INFLUENCES THAT YOU DIDN'T KNOW WERE PUNK AS FUCK

By Shari Page

I GOT THE IDEA to become a drummer after my mom took me to an activity fair on Long Island. There were different hobbies to choose from: dance, karate, soccer, Girl Scouts, etc. My mom mentioned drum lessons as we walked by the table belonging to the Long Island Drum Center. As a third grader in the nineties, I was already obsessed with music. I would stay up all night watching music videos on MTV and dreamed of being in a band—even if it was a pop group on *TRL*. At that moment, drumming became the only option.

My parents supported the lessons but wouldn't buy me a kit due to the noise. I printed out pictures of drum sets and left them all over the house, hoping mom and dad would catch the hint. I finally scraped together enough babysitting money to buy an old dusty used drum kit. I think it was a Hohner.

Years later, I found myself looking for gigs on Craigslist. I stumbled across an ad titled "Two Girls One Drummer." That was the start of our band THICK.

Sheila E.
Solo Artist, Prince

I remember when I first saw Sheila E. do a drum solo on *The Late Show with David Letterman* wearing high heels, I was in awe of how badass it was. Even though I play drums barefoot, I have a deep appreciation for someone who can shred the drums in high heels...I can't even walk in heels. When I saw other videos of Sheila E. playing her drum solos during that time (no pun intended, for Prince's *Sign O' the Times*), every hit was more punk than the next. There were enough rack toms to fill a room, and the shredding, rhythm, funk, punk, and feel was next level. If you sped up these drum fills, even faster than they are already played, you would get one hectic punk rock song.

Karen Carpenter
The Carpenters

One of the best things about the Carpenters is that they performed on their own variety TV show with skits, music, and most importantly...Karen Carpenter playing insane drum solos. *The Carpenters' Very First TV Special* from 1976 features a marching band skit where Karen is told, "Besides, girls don't play drums anyways." Then it shows her playing a snare marching solo before absolutely shredding a full drum kit. Next, she moves to standing rack toms and bongos for another fantastic drum solo. Then, she's back to slaying the drum set. What I admire about her style is how fast she can play without missing a beat. It doesn't get more punk rock than being told drums aren't for girls and then playing a fantastic solo on multiple different drums.

Thomas Pridgen
The Mars Volta

When I saw the Mars Volta play live, it was such a surreal experience...and not just because I caught Thomas Pridgen's drumstick after their set. Every song had such heavy drumming with fills that traveled at the speed of light. Thomas brings such a punk aesthetic to his crazy drumming style. There is so much feel and movement happening at once that it's like a performance within a performance. Some songs to check out are "Metatron," "Wax Simulacra," and "Soothsayer."

Stella Mozgawa
Warpaint

Warpaint has been one of my favorite bands for the last ten years, and I even committed to seeing them a few years ago with a bad fever. Stella is one of those drummers that has so much feel and punk energy that it's jaw dropping. I would say Stella has BPE, big punk energy. She is the type of drummer that slams on the ride cymbal and it holds the energy of every punk band in one hit. Her heavy and rhythmic smashing really brings the punk rock to Warpaint's ambient, trippy songs. Some of my favorite Warpaint drum tracks are on "Composure," "Hi," and "Above Control."

Travis Barker
Blink-182

We all know Travis is "punk as fuck," but I saved the best for last. He's my ultimate drumming hero. I grew up obsessed with Blink-182, and I would even try to talk like I was from Southern California (I'm from Long Island). I would come home from school every day and play drums to every Blink-182 song. I was obsessed with the way he held his drumsticks, the way he played such fast drum fills, and his punk-rock beats that were almost too perfect for punk. I love drummers who have a distinctive style, and if Travis is drumming you immediately know who it is. He plays so fast that you might miss one of his enigmatic drum fills if you aren't paying attention. My favorite Blink-182 drum tracks are on "Aliens Exist," "Shut Up," "Rock Show," "Down," and "Reckless Abandon."

Shari Page *is the drummer for the band THICK. She first took drum lessons during elementary school after attending an activity fair with her mom on Long Island. She picked drumming up again as a tween and bought her first drum set with babysitting money. She met her future bandmates in THICK after seeing a Craigslist ad titled "Two Girls One Drummer."*

REGGAE, HARDCORE, & DEATH

By Urian Hackney

M Y INTRODUCTION TO PUNK and drumming was by destroying my brothers' seven-inches and CDs (sorry dudes), the reggae scene, and my father and uncles.

From the eighties until the mid-aughts, my dad played in a reggae band called Lambsbread. They were at the peak of success and a well-known group in the reggae scene when I was still a baby. Mikey Dread, Burning Spear, Black Uhuru, Steel Pulse, Augustus Pablo, and many more were peers and good family friends at the time. That's where my interest in drumming started to grow.

When I was about four, my parents got me my first guitar. Unbeknownst to them, I was a lefty, but they bought me a right-handed guitar. I tried my best to play it, but it never clicked. My father and uncle—who lives downstairs from my family—built a project studio next to our house where Lambsread practiced. I remember giving myself pep talks, working up the courage to go downstairs and ask my uncle to play his seemingly monstrous kit. The cool thing at that time in the reggae scene was Simmons electronic drums. They looked and sounded like something out of a Voltron comic. Quite honestly, if you were in a reggae band and you didn't have Simmons drums, you didn't mean shit to me. All the greats had them, including my uncle Dannis.

Sitting behind that kit made me feel like I was in the cockpit of the world's coolest robot. As a six-year-old, my influences were Carlton Barrett (Bob Marley & the Wailers), Leroy "Horsemouth" Wallace (the Gladiators, Burning Spear), and Sly Dunbar (Sly and Robbie). While I had that exposure to reggae, I was also surrounded by skateboarding and punk. At one point in time, me and my two older brothers all lived together in the same room. Our oldest brother, Bobby, got into punk and hardcore through skating and it trickled down to me and Jules. I remember scouring through his seven-inches while he was gone at work (definitely stood on and spun around on a Judge record and got my ass kicked for it). Eventually, I got into skating too and started to develop tastes of my own. Thankfully, Bobby was enthusiastic and actually helped me out. He was playing in a bunch of punk and hardcore bands during that time. My favorite of those bands was called In Reach. I always thought my brother's drums sounded perfect and the fills are still ingrained in my playing today.

Some words of wisdom that trickled down from my uncle Dannis—to Bobby first and then to me—was to always hit the kick when you crash the cymbals. He had a green Pearl Export drum kit that made the rounds to just about every one of our bands (Rough Francis included) and was cool to let me borrow them for gigs when I needed them.

For my eleventh birthday, my brother Jules handed me a red CD with a picture of a bald dude screaming into a microphone on the cover—the Minor Threat discography. I remember asking my parents for a drum set for my birthday as well, but I knew that was a little unrealistic since I shared a room with my brother in our small house, and we didn't have very much money. I was lucky that year though, because they did buy me a practice pad kit. The hardware and pads on the kit reminded me of my uncle's

Simmons Voltron kit, but without the electronics. I spent many days locked in my darkened room with a hand me down Discman and those practice pads, trying my best to keep up with Minor Threat's drummer, Jeff Nelson. That made me more aware of drumming in music and was the first time I felt like I was forming my own taste in music.

I got heavy into drummers like Earl Hudson [Bad Brains], Tommy Ramone [Ramones], Keith Moon [the Who; the movie *Tommy* was a staple in my house], Mitch Mitchell [the Jimi Hendrix Experience], Clyde Stubblefield [James Brown, Aretha Franklin], Robo [Black Flag], and Bill Stevenson [Descendents]. My favorite songs to play by those drummers and bands included "Right Brigade," "Rock 'n' Roll High School," "Boris the Spider," "Manic Depression," "Lickin' Stick," and "Jealous Again." My first band was a hardcore outfit called Punchout with my older brother Jules on vocals and some of his buddies from around town and friends from 242 Main in Burlington, Vermont. Right before our first show, me and my friends broke into a middle school right next to our house and tripped the silent alarm. We actually ended up getting a key from a younger janitor we befriended who didn't feel like he was getting paid enough. We raided the cafeteria of its ice cream sandwiches and snacks and skated the picnic tables out front.

We eventually got caught (this was my first local newspaper debut!), and I had to do a pretty extensive number of chores and get convincing from my older bandmates to play that show. It was an opening slot for Murphy's Law. I was thirteen at the time and their lead singer, Jimmy G., gave me a lighter with a pot leaf on it and told me to "go light some shit on fire." Unfortunately, my dad took it and lit his own shit on fire.

The bass player for Punchout, Jeff Foran, and the guitar player that eventually played for Rough Francis, Paul Comegno, started their own non-hardcore project called Maneuvers. I tried out and it was my first experience playing rock. That's when I discovered more modern drummers like Mario Rubalcaba [OFF!, Earthless], John Theodore [The Mars Volta, Queens of the Stone Age], and Joey Castillo [Queens of the Stone Age, Danzig]. But I didn't discover two of the most important bands and drummers in my life until my mid-teens—Scott Asheton of the Stooges and Dennis "Machine Gun" Thompson of MC5.

The striking thing about both bands was their simplicity and familiarity. My parents were a little younger than me when they discovered those same bands, stumbling onto them in the late sixties at shows opening for Grand Funk Railroad and Alice Cooper at the Grande Ballroom in Detroit—but I didn't know that then. When I first heard them, it was as poignant as the first time I had sex. So simple, primal, and sleazy, with a rhythm that felt like you were on the ground getting kicked in the head over and over. This discovery encouraged me to travel backward and discover other drummers like Tony Williams [Miles Davis, the Tony Williams Lifetime], Jaki Liebezeit [Can], and Charles Connor [Little Richard].

This was also around the time I discovered my father was once in a punk band in Detroit himself called Death. Maneuvers used to record demos on a reel to reel, and my father had some 1/4" master reels from a session at United Sound in Detroit. He asked if he could borrow that tape deck to transfer the tape. The machine wasn't calibrated, so the transfers were a little faster than modern masters. I remember hearing it for the first time and being so excited, confused, and amazed. I was taking a shit, and the project studio roof is adjacent to the window in the bathroom. It was normal to hear reggae shaking the house from his control room, but this time it was punk. Hearing my dad play these "tapes from when he was a kid" made me lose my shit (no pun intended). Did he secretly listen to punk? Was he hiding something from us? I had so many thoughts and questions racing through my head. There were many times he talked about playing in a band that sounded like the punk I listened to, but I shrugged it off because he was always a reggae guy to me. I had a hard time believing it when I found out his old band played the kind of punk rock that my brothers and I got into (you're telling me the guys who played punk before it was a thing are the same dudes telling me to mow the lawn, stack wood, and do chores?), but it reassured me in the path I was already on.

At that point, me, Bobby, and Jules all played in a band called From the Ground Up. Jules played bass and Bobby played drums. Then when Bobby left the band, I ended up playing drums. A few years later, Bobby, Jules, Alan Blackman (of FTGU), and I were in a Halloween Bad Brains cover band (called Three Hackney's and a Blackman) and that was the first time the three of us played together. Once the word got around about Death, two of our other friends, Steve Williams and Dylan Giambatista, joined on guitar and bass and started Rough Francis (named in honor of our late uncle Dave, who was the main songwriter and spiritual compass for Death). We wanted to become missionaries and play this record that no one had ever heard before. I vividly remember learning my uncle Dannis' beats for the first time, especially "Politicians in My Eyes," and thinking how everything he played was the embodiment of punk. He had the speed, the simplicity, and the ferociousness, and this legend was living right below my bedroom all these years.

Rough Francis played Death tunes at a handful of shows. That was until Mickey Leigh (Joey Ramone's older brother) reached out and asked us to open for Fishbone at the Filmore

East in New York—but they wanted Death on the bill as well. At the time, Lambsbread was still active as a three-piece, so they started relearning the Death stuff for the first time in thirty years. Ever since that first reunion show, they've reestablished themselves as a band, touring the world for the first time ever. Every now and again we still cover their songs, but Death started playing again, and we were eager to let them do their thing and establish our own sound. With this newly discovered punk lineage, my brothers Bobby, Jules, and I started digging into the music that inspired my dad and his brothers, as well as unearthing our punk and hardcore roots to create what Rough Francis is today.

Urian Hackney *is the drummer from Rough Francis and The Armed, and has filled in for hardcore punk bands Burn, and Converge. Urian is also an audio engineer at a Vermont based recording studio, The Box, and is the son of Bobby Hackney, founder of proto punk band DEATH.*

RAT SCABIES OF THE DAMNED

Interviewed by S. W. Lauden

I KNEW CERTAIN PATTERNS and themes would emerge as I put this collection together. So, it was no surprise when many contributors name-checked the Damned's Rat Scabies. He and guitarist Brian James founded the band in 1976, quickly adding vocalist Dave Vanian and bassist Captain Sensible to form the original line up. The Damned was the first UK punk band to release a single, "New Rose," and the first of their peers to tour the US. Scabies played with the Damned (in various line ups and musical phases) through 1995, on eight studio albums including the punk classics, *Damned Damned Damned* (1977) and *Machine Gun Etiquette* (1979).

Let's give Rat Scabies the last word...

When did you start playing drums?

I fell in love with the drums when I was about eight, the sound of the toms and cymbals. It's that moment when you have a reaction to something and it just takes over. There's no real logic to it, it just kind of bites in. I wanted to be a drummer, so I did everything possible to get close to it. But it was much harder then, because you couldn't go get lessons. I was ten or eleven years old trying to find somebody to teach me, but nobody wanted to. So, I joined the school orchestra, which immediately gave me a trumpet; then I joined the Sea Cadets, which immediately gave me a cornet. I was like, "I want to be a drummer!" And they were like, "Cornet players are what we need. Everybody wants to be a drummer." But I was lucky in a way—I didn't learn how to read music, but I got an understanding of how notes worked.

Who were some early drumming influences?

Anything with a lot of drums. There was a lot of jazz when I was a kid and, as I never tire of saying, jazz is great because there's a drum solo in every song. So, there was always something for me to look forward to. I had a great big band album with Gene Krupa on it, and some Glen Miller stuff. Anything that was overly percussive, that's what I wanted.

If I didn't have to play with other musicians, I never would have done so—what would be the point? But at a certain point I listened to Sandy Nelson and realized even he, a guy who played tunes on tom-toms, had a guitarist. It was a sudden realization that maybe the rest of the world didn't love drums quite as much as I did, and that maybe you needed to have something else going on until the next big drum moment.

It's interesting you mention Gene Krupa, since he was a big influence on Jerry Nolan from the New York Dolls and the Heartbreakers.

The thing about Krupa was he was attainable. You could hear what Krupa did and it was musical, it made sense. As opposed to his archrival, Buddy Rich, who was just terrifying. You'd hear him play and you'd be like "I'm going to go burn these sticks now. Why did I ever think I could do any of this?!" With Krupa, you can just listen. Same thing with Sandy Nelson, it's that ability to bring melody out of the drum kit.

A lot of other realizations come out of that, especially with Krupa. For him, it was all about playing with the band and supporting what's going on around you. When you get those four bars, twirl your sticks, and make it look fucking great, show off as much as you can, and then go back to playing the song. Krupa single-handedly made it seem like the drummer held the whole band together.

So, I would say Krupa was always the bigger influence on punk drummers. Which is why I think punk sustained so long, it's the simplicity. If it's too difficult or too technical, you just get disheartened as a beginner. If you pick up a guitar, you can play a Ramones song in as many minutes as it takes to listen to it. That inspires people to keep going and go on to bigger and better things eventually. There's a lot to be said for it being dumb. [Laughs]

How did you make the transition from listening to jazz to what eventually became punk?

I could never play jazz. It was something that was always beyond me. I can just about bluff my way through it now, but it was always just sort of around. Then, after jazz, everything became blues. Mitch Mitchell, John Bonham—all those guys were jazz drummers. I mean, Keith Moon was probably the only one who wasn't. The blues explosion was all about the guitar, but later on you started to get the drummer and guitarist combos where there was complete empathy between the two—Jimmy Page and John Bonham [Led Zeppelin], Pete Townsend and Keith Moon [the Who], Eric Clapton and Ginger Baker [Cream]. And those were the bands that were big at the time, so when the Damned got going, I think it was very logical that Brian James and I were in that headspace.

It's been said that American bands like the New York Dolls, the Ramones, and the Stooges had a big influence on early English punk. Was that true in your personal experience?

I kind of lived under a rock. I was suburban. I'd heard of the New York Dolls and the Stooges. I think I'd seen both of them on TV once and they were kind of okay, but what made me go "wow" were MC5. There was something about Dennis Thompson, his timing, and those machine gun snare rolls. I could never do it. I tried and tried, but there's just something about the way he did that.

Brian James, however, was very clued up on those guys. Especially their attitude—this idea that perfection is over-rated. So, Dennis Thompson was a favorite, but Tommy Ramone was *the* guy for me. The way he put his parts together was absolutely perfect. Again, playing the tune.

And he wasn't even a "real drummer."

Shhhhhh! You'll ruin everything.

Who were some of your favorite drummers among your early English punk peers?

I always really liked the way Paul Cook [Sex Pistols] played. Something about the way he went about it, he was rock solid and always played the right things in the right places. And I always liked what Jet Black [the Stranglers] did, because what he played was always kind of interesting. It wasn't necessarily my style, but that guy knew what he was doing. And then Topper Headon [the Clash], of course, could always play full stop. I was the guy who flailed around a lot, but Topper was always solid. He's very Jim Keltner in a way. I'm sure I've left a few people out. Then I marched in and was like, "Get out of my way! I'll show you how this is done. This is what drums are for." [Laughs]

I think there was still this element of musicians wanting to be taken seriously by their peers and the audience at the time. Whereas I think the Damned didn't really have anything to lose. We knew a lot of people weren't going to get it, but, for some reason, that was what we were going to do. I always felt like we were doomed to failure, but what did I know? I loved playing with Brian, and I loved Dave and the Captain and being in a band with them, but, you know, I thought it was going to last about three months. I thought, "Nobody's going to like this. It's not like anything else out there, so of course nobody is going to buy this."

Your drumming progresses rapidly over the first three albums, from the raw sixties garage beats on Damned Damned Damned *to the much more dynamic playing on* Machine Gun Etiquette. *Were you aware of that at the time, or was it all happening too fast?*

By the time we got to *Machine Gun Etiquette,* we were ready for a different approach to what we did. We didn't just want to be a three-chord punk band that repeated the same formula on every record. We enjoyed the whole creative process and trying something like the piano on the beginning of "Melody Lee." I remember Captain saying that he didn't know if the punters would like it because it was a bit slow. I was like, "It's okay, it doesn't last for long. They'll forgive us. Just as long as we suddenly speed it up, they'll be good with it." We realized that with things like the intro to "Smash It Up," too. And our audience were actually ready to move along at the same pace we were, which was our saving grace because if they weren't we'd have been high and dry.

You don't start playing music so you can do the same thing for the rest of your life. It's one of those sad ironies that you go on stage and people really only want to hear your previous work. They don't want to hear anything new because it's not established, but you can't establish it because nobody wants to hear anything new. So, it does sort of go against you in that sense. But I couldn't stay the same. This is why I always tried to get involved in projects that people didn't think would suit me or that you wouldn't think I would do, because I like the challenge of having to play with Donovan. Suddenly everything's very quiet, and it's "Mellow Yellow," but it's a challenging thing to do. It's all part of what being a musician is.

It's like Bowie said, if you can push a musician a little out of their comfort zone, then the end results are far more interesting. You've got the choice, you can either take a run and flying leap at it and hope for genius and brilliance, or you can fall flat on your face like some complete cunt. You've always got a fifty-fifty chance, so I always take the flier if I can…and hope to be held up as a genius. But the truth is it's just another bluff.

From the perspective of somebody who was there from the start, and still playing today, what do you make of the many ways punk has evolved and mutated over the decades?

I think the most interesting thing about punk's mutations is that everybody seems to have a different idea of what punk is. I swear, the next fucker who tries to tell me what "punk rock ethics" are, I'm going to fucking punch them. I've heard it all, but in a funny way they're all right. Everybody takes the bit they like best and presents it as the thing punk was built on. But the truth is it was built on sand, it was built on absolutely nothing. And in a literal sense. We had nothing, so we made clothes ourselves—we'd wear bin-liners and dog collars. Society didn't have room for us, and we couldn't afford their society. If you give us nothing, that is what you're going to get back. And we gave them nothing by the bucket-load.

But I do like the way punk ethics rubbed off on a lot of bands. Like Green Day. I met them very early on in their career and thought they sounded a bit like the Clash. Then I went to see them a couple of years ago in London and they were fucking brilliant. They're just so good at what they do.

Punk drumming has undergone some radical stylistic changes over the last couple decades. Is modern punk music recognizable to you?

It's all technique. I listen to speed metal bands and wonder how they do that with their feet. Some of what these guys do is fucking incredible. It's beyond Buddy Rich. It's another method, another trick that you can master. What I do find really interesting is that there's a lot more going on with arrangements now. I think performance has kind of reached its peak.

But the thing about technical players is that you're always really impressed by their brilliance, until you go into the next club where there's a very similar drummer doing very similar things. There's no uniqueness in that. So, you end up with two schools. There's [technical mastery], or you can try to push your imagination as far as it will go—which always sounds fucked up because it's new and different because nobody has anything to compare it to.

Do you see any connection to what was happening in the seventies?

There isn't a connection, really. What we did was blood and sweat. Nobody taught me how to do a one-handed roll. Like I said, you couldn't get lessons, so you learned to play on pillows and cushions. Everything was single stroke. If you used technique, it was much quieter and didn't really count for much. And years later, you realize how right you were when a recording engineer puts a noise gate on your snare. It's like, "I spent two years learning how to do that paradiddle flam ghost and you gated it out." And the engineer's like, "I just want it to go 'crack.' I don't need all that frilly stuff, it's just getting in the way." I think it's very easy to waste a lot of time doing things that never get heard.

Any advice for a young drummer looking to start their first punk band?

The only advice I ever give anyone is to make sure you do it with people you like. You can always teach somebody to play, but you can't teach them to be fun, or have ideas, or think laterally.

And only ever please yourself. Make records that you want to make, that you think sound good, and not because you think it should sound like your biggest influence. It's really important that you please yourself and do it with people you can hang out with because you'll end up sitting next to them in the back of a tour van for nine hours, so you better be able to talk to them.